Consciously Creating
Wealth

The Secret for Wealth, Wisdom, & Success

CODY HORTON

Dedication

My Deepest Love and Appreciation

To my lovable and creative husband Douglas, for your *invaluable* strength and caring, and for sharing this grand adventure of life with me!

To my extraordinary friend Linda Joy, for your *genuine* love, joy, humor, and incredible sparkle!

To my marvelous friend Barbara Jean, for your heart of *pure* gold, boundless love and impish wit!

To my magnificent friend Dan, for your *authentic* interest in others, your thoughtfulness and generosity!

To my funny father Bill, for teaching me that I can do anything I set my *heart* on!

To my musical mother Willie, for telling me to look *inside* for the answers!

To the Spirit within, you are the *wisdom*, and the *inspiration* in us all!

Contents

Notes

Introduction

"Yes! Ready money is Aladdin's lamp."
–Lord Byron

Riches, wealth, happiness and success are all achieved by tapping into the magical power of your own mind. We are just beginning to understand the tremendous power of the mind and by knowing how to use the many facets of the mind, the conscious as well as the subconscious, you can achieve whatever you want! Everything that you desire has been put here for you to use and enjoy. If not, why is it here? Unfortunately, most people do not realize the unlimited potential they have, so they lead lives that are limited and impoverished.

You have the ability and the power to reach your unfulfilled dreams, because you are the *master* of your own destiny, and you can make your life anything you wish it to be. As you begin using the magical powers of your mind, you will experience great changes, and nothing will be impossible for you anymore!

What type of feeling emerges when you see the words wealth, success or money? Is it a good feeling or a feeling of resentment and envy? Do any of the following statements reflect how you feel?

- ❑ People who are wealthy have come by it dishonestly.
- ❑ Money is the root of all evil.
- ❑ I have a special gift to help others, but I can't take money for using it.
- ❑ I am always in debt.
- ❑ I have to work hard just to make ends meet.
- ❑ No one can be spiritual and wealthy, too.
- ❑ Everyone else has more wealth then me.
- ❑ Oh! I could never pay that much for _____!

(You fill in the blank)

How could any of the above statements create abundance, success or prosperity?

Our role models were very powerful teachers for us. What events concerning wealth were impressed upon you that later became housed in your subconscious [or as I like to call it, the creative mind]? What we witnessed and learned as children we believed to be true, and over time the creative mind became conditioned to follow in our role model's footsteps. Think back to some of the comments you heard from respected persons in your life. You may have heard that you are always lucky, you are creative, you will be the greatest success in the world, or how in the world do you expect to get ahead and is this the best you can do? If you believed any of these comments, then events in your life would inevitably turn out the way you were shown, either in the positive or negative sense.

Studies show that individuals have a 67% chance of having the same habits as their parents, even if they disapprove of the habits. Perceptions become ingrained subliminally and condition the creative mind, so it goes about setting the same course for us. Until you become consciously aware, the creative mind is busy night and day and seems to perform its work independently from your conscious perception. At the core of your creative mind are the beliefs, emotions and feelings you have about life such as happiness, enthusiasm, anger, or sadness. The creative mind houses images and perceptions that you have about yourself, i.e., perceptions about how successful you can be, the nature of your health, what your feeling is about wealth, what sort of family you will have or even the amount of love you feel you deserve. These ideas and beliefs are important because they direct your life and what your creative mind believes and feels, you become. If your creative mind believes that you deserve a successful and happy life, chances are, you will have one. The creative mind directs you to behave in such a way as to achieve your goals.

The creative mind is not however, as many would believe, separate from the conscious mind, but rather an integral part of it. The conscious mind is the portion, which analyzes, rationalizes and is logical. Many therapists would have us believe that we are helpless to change the creative mind and are at the mercy of a creative force we do not understand. The creative mind may seem to hold invisible beliefs but when you consciously begin to examine the contents of your mind, you will find the beliefs have always been there, but you just became aware of them. The conscious mind not only interprets your outer environment, but is conscious of your inner beliefs as well, and initially gives the creative mind information on how to direct activity. The information that you take in through the conscious mind permeates the creative mind, which in turn automatically influences the conscious mind. The ability of the conscious mind to make decisions and establish direction is of great value, however it must be done with awareness to create a fulfilled life. It is meant not only to interpret circumstances in the outer environment but also your feelings and thoughts within. It works by extrapolating information inside and out so that when you do make decisions, you have the full spectrum of information available to you. Your reality is none other then the product of your feelings and thoughts, conscious or not.

Even though the mind is infinitely greater then any computer man can make, let's use it as a metaphor; your conscious mind is used for the input of material and the creative mind is the software that is programmed. If the programming is excellent, then the output is positive; if the input is faulty, then problems occur. Individuals behave in ways that reflect their deepest beliefs and most individuals have never consciously taken the time to examine what they think or believe. If one harbor's fears of failure, low self-esteem and inadequacy, then that person will maintain a life that verifies those feelings. However, if a person has consciously examined their beliefs, worked on their self-image and maintained a positive attitude, then their life reflects those feelings.

Just as water will reach its own level by its own weight, the same will happen with our thoughts about money and wealth. Whatever we feel we deserve, that is precisely what we will get. Even if money were to fall into our laps and we felt we didn't deserve it, it would quickly leave our lives. Have you read, heard or thought you should *only* be desirous of money to help others? Please understand that this type of thinking is erroneous because it is stating that you are not worthy of money, only others are. We cannot give what we ourselves do not have. It seems that the majority of people have issues surrounding money! They feel uncomfortable even discussing the topic of money because deep down inside they feel it is wrong. If you have no interest in money, then how do you expect to attract it? Many individuals associate wealth with greed and avarice; they feel that money has somehow been the cause of many problems. The truth however, is that prosperity was achieved prior to a wealthy person understanding or acknowledging their spirituality. Greed is the belief in lack and that there is not enough to go around. It is the *belief* that is the cause behind the attachment to money for a sense of security. An enlightened individual is taught to accept the abundance of life with non-attachment thereby creating a balance between spirituality and riches. Non-attachment does not equal indifference either!

> "A feast is made for laughter and wine maketh merry,
> but money answereth all things."
> –Ecclesiastes 10:19

Wealth in the form of money is used only as a medium of exchange. In and of itself, money is neither good nor bad, but what we choose to do with it. In early times people tried many different types of exchange, so money took on many fascinating forms such as tin, iron, cattle, platinum, tobacco, soap, seashells, nails, tea, salt, feathers, bones, as well as gold. What is all this intense negative energy surrounding the form of exchange that we use? Even though money is one of the simplest things to come by, to a great number of people, it is the most elusive. Money is the one thing they never have enough of!

You can express more of life and help more people with wealth then you can without it. Poverty is not a blessing, abundance is our birthright and when we consciously realize this, we can better understand how it is to thrive and be creative rather then to use precious energies just to survive.

Now, as you continue on the path of wealth and abundance, keep an open heart and an open mind. Those of you who are open and willing to learn will contribute much to your advancement and happiness. If some of this information doesn't make sense to you, don't force yourself to understand or accept it, just let it settle in and in time it will become clearer to you. Even if you don't believe some of the information, this will not make it any less true. When your conscious awareness increases, the lessons contained herein will become *very* valuable to you. Those of you, who think you know everything or approach this subject with doubt and resistance, will learn very little or nothing. For this very reason, the sages concealed much of this profound knowledge, because they recognized the limitations of prejudiced thinking.

The exercises throughout this book are designed to encourage increased concentration, refine your skills of perception, improve your intuition and stimulate your creative mind. You will gain awareness of how you feel about wealth and how you can make the changes you want. Also, you will increase your level of understanding, and come to know that the unusual things that frequently happen to you are not just mere coincidences. For your greatest good, be neutral in your thinking and be determined to gain all the benefits from the information that is being given to you.

Life truly is magical and extraordinary, so prepare yourself for an enchanted journey. When you master these secrets; success, wealth, and happiness will abound in your life beyond your wildest dreams!

What Are My Feelings About Wealth?

1. How did my parents or role models influence my beliefs about wealth, directly or indirectly, as I was growing up? What did they teach me about money? _____

   _____

2. What type of inner conversation about wealth do I have with myself? Is it positive or negative?_____

   _____

   _____

3. Do I take time to appreciate and love all the wealth, great relationships and good things I have in my life right now? If not, why not? _____

   _____

   _____

4. Do my opinions about wealth differ from those of my family, friends or mate? If so, how?_____

   _____

FOR MONEY OR AGAINST MONEY

This exercise increases your awareness about your beliefs surrounding money.

Fold the paper in half, and list reasons *FOR* having money. Then, on the right side, list reasons *AGAINST* having money.

Are these individual or universal beliefs? What beliefs are you holding onto that no longer serve you?

FOR

AGAINST

1

It's
Your
Imagination!

"What is now proved was once only imagin'd."
–William Blake

We have the power to be anything we desire if we just use our imagination consciously. We use our imagination all the time, but most of the time we are not conscious of what we are imagining for ourselves.

You must, however, discern between reality and imagination in order to live in this world effectively. But your reality does spring *from* your imagination which began because of your beliefs. Imagination wakes all the subtle forces of nature, and the creative power of your mind.

The dictionary defines imagination as gifted with the creative faculty or to form in the mind an idea or image. How does this apply to us? Through imagination we create from within and bring about what we want into the physical world of objects. Imagination takes us into the world of the unknown – a world of supertemporal probabilities.

Most individuals do not trust their imagination because it doesn't deal in fact, when in truth it is precisely what you have imagined that created the events in your life.

The following story illustrates how effective using your imagination can be. My husband and I were both laid off from our jobs at the same time. We were among the first to feel the impact of large corporations downsizing. We had a huge house payment, luxury car payments and more. We thought we had no choice but to sell our home and possessions, so we would have money to live on. We had not learned the techniques for wealth yet, so we succumbed to the "poor me" trap. We went through our money very fast and were down to our last twenty five hundred dollars. I began reading several prosperity books, literally anything I could get my hands on to show us how to create abundance. We applied some of the techniques that I had read about, and also some that I felt intuitively would work.

One day we were sitting in a restaurant in downtown Denver, and looked across the street to a quaint area filled with specialty shops. My husband said that it would be great to have a man's custom clothing shop in that area. After

3

lunch we walked over to see if there was space available; we were told *absolutely* nothing was for lease and nothing was anticipated. We went home, and began imagining that we had already opened a shop in that particular area. In the interim, I went to the library to research names of tailors in the United States that we could order fabric samples from and to gain knowledge about measuring individuals for custom shirts and suits. The companies we contacted each sent out a representative to teach us what we needed to learn to start a custom clothing business. There was no charge for the samples or the training, however we did have to guarantee a certain amount of business for the companies to supply us with materials. We continued to imagine owning our own shop for approximately another three weeks when suddenly I felt a desire to call again and inquire about space for lease. It turned out, the space we wanted was available, as the previous tenant decided not to renew their lease. The management gave us three days to decide if we wanted the space, so we acted immediately and had them draw up the lease. The deposit was two thousand dollars (just what we had left), and we were given one month's free rent, allowing us time to bring in money through sales. From there our business increased to approximately $300,000 in just the second year of operation. All this came about because we *imagined* owning a shop and acted upon our *desire*. Creative expression and major clues to create solutions for any challenges you may encounter, stem *from* your imagination.

> "Imagination is not a talent of some men
> but is the health of every man."
> –Ralph Waldo Emerson

Reality depends on the use of your imagination not on some external factor. Do not get stuck in the so-called "rational" way of thinking, because your creative mind does not work in a "rational" way. Reality cannot be confined to the limited boundaries of the intellect. Imagination has no limitations and through your imagination you can escape the limitation of your self-imposed thinking. Nothing can stop you, except what you are imagining for yourself!

When we awaken to the fact that we create all the time and that we create our reality by the use of our imagination, we will begin to consciously think about what we really want. You often cannot see the correlation between your thoughts, expectations, desires, and the events you experience that are seemingly outside of your control. You compose your life experience and you are intimately connected with your environment, and any physical event that you experience. You literally give birth to your experiences! Reality becomes what you imagine intertwined with belief; it is the outer projection of your imagination. Your creative mind and imagination must be consciously exercised and directed. If you are experiencing something in your life that you don't like, change it by imagining something different. If you consciously evaluate what you have been imagining for yourself, you may be quite surprised. You either imagined that you didn't deserve something better or imagined something terrible happening to you or you didn't listen to that inner voice – your intuition trying to catch your attention to guide you in the right direction.

To align with this tremendous power, you have only to come to the realization that you create your reality and everything you have in your life has come *from* what you imagined. Nothing appears or continues in appearance on its own. You had to imagine certain events because what you experience has no power of its own, therefore events continue because you are imagining them.

> "Imagination is more important than knowledge."
> –Albert Einstein

This first secret to consciously creating wealth is an extraordinary gift. Begin by changing what you imagine for yourself and then you will see a change in your experiences. The creative mind does not know the difference from an imagined or real event, so this shows that you have the ability to consciously influence it. Our world is not mechanistic – it is purely imaginal and Einstein understood this!

You cannot change your reality if you only identify with what is already seen. You'll want to consciously begin the process of change by not identifying with outer appearances. Reality has its roots in the imagination – the unseen world. We have to look inward and imagine a new set of circumstances for ourselves. Put your whole trust in the feeling that your dreams are already fulfilled and pay no attention to physical events right now. By becoming aware of what you want and consciously using your imagination, your desires will become a reality and you will begin to experience more control over your life.

> "Imagination disposes of everything,
> it creates beauty, justice, and happiness,
> which are everything in this world."
> –Blaise Pascal

We must think *from* and not *of* what we want in our life. The rich man, poor man, beggar man or thief are all experiencing reality *from* what they have imagined for themselves. Use the law of imagination wisely, because if you say you are poor, your creative mind immediately begins to create the conditions for poverty. If you were to contradict this in your conscious mind, you would stop the action, but most people are not that aware of their thoughts and their reality mirror's back the condition they have been imagining *from*. Imagination reflects and being creative, reflects back to us exactly what we have been imagining. Imagine your reality *from* the state of consciousness that your desires are already fulfilled and they will become real. Use your imagination consciously to create the desirable and to transform the undesirable.

Do not intellectualize how the events will take place, rather imagine them *from* the end result, and allow your creative mind to handle the details. Many times I have thought *of* what I wanted in my life, intellectualized how it was to happen and then nothing happened. I was always thinking *from* a limited perspective and that is exactly what I received – *limitation*!

"Imagination, which in truth, is
but another name for absolute power.
And clearest insight, amplitude of mind
and reason in her most exalted mood."
–William Wordsworth

You live in a world of infinite opportunities and you create with what you imagine yourself to be, so why not imagine the grandest events for yourself!

Imagine *from* your desired state at least once a day, and you will see your dreams come true. All my experiences have convinced me of this truth. Experiment with your imagination until these secrets become your own. Your accomplishments will be the proof of your power to create through your imagination!

We are free to imagine what we want, so take a moment and consciously think about what you have been imagining for yourself. What we imagine right now, in the present moment, is creating our future. What we have imagined in the past has created the circumstances we are now experiencing in our lives, even at this precise moment. If you knew this to the very depth of your soul, you would consciously begin working with your imagination to create the reality you want.

Many individuals have said to me that it must be fate or destiny when something happens to them that they didn't want to undergo. They feel that there must be some hidden message in it for them. Yes! There is a message and that is to take responsibility for your life and know that you have created the circumstances you are now experiencing. Begin by living in the present moment, and to be consciously aware of your thoughts. If you don't choose for yourself then you will experience whatever life brings to you. It is the lack of direction in your life that creates the misery you experience, so be focused in your imagination and think *from* already living your dream. You have to consciously make the effort to control the process of your thoughts and to use your imagination intelligently! At first you may find this difficult and you may even become discouraged, but this is the *very* time you must remain focused. Even if you fall backward, the more you realize that your thoughts and imagination create your reality, you will experience greater and greater good in your life. However, this takes a person with courage!

"Science does not know its debt to imagination."
–Ralph Waldo Emerson

Ignorance of the ability to imagine what you want and imagine your desires fulfilled, keeps you limited and underestimates the ability that you have to create what you want in your life. The creative mind is put into action by consciously using your imagination (a subjective state of mind) which brings about your objective reality (what you experience in your life). All that matters to the creative mind is what you imagine yourself to be!

Images are considered thought and when you think *from* having your desires fulfilled, you put your creative mind to work. Imagine an event that is as natural to yourself as it can be. You want life to reflect you by imagining what you want and if you have no idea of what you want, then you merely reflect life. Your life can be a grand adventure if you will just use your imagination creatively – dare to dream!

"All you behold, tho' it appears without,
it is within, in your Imagination."
–Blake

The creative mind is always reflecting what you are imagining, and since you are constantly creating, through imagination you can escape the known. You can go beyond the limitations of the senses and the realm of reason. Remember, you continue to keep the past in existence and create your future by sustaining the events through your imagination. It doesn't matter what has happened in the past – the only thing that is important, is what you think right now!

One of my students remarked that he thought this theory had him presenting himself better than he was. The fact is, imagination is always shaping our lives, and he needed to understand that he was experiencing exactly what he had imagined himself to be. You are not to go around in your physical reality pretending you are something you are not, instead use the power of your imagination until you have created the change in your outer experiences. The cause of existence begins first within the imagination. My student believed that his experiences were beyond his control when in truth, he was experiencing exactly what he had created with his imagination. He attended the "Consciously Creating Wealth" workshop because he was always broke. At the beginning of every month he was always frantic, because he never had enough money for his rent; his wife told me the first thing he said was, "See, I told you so"! He kept imagining that he wouldn't be able to pay his rent on time, and it became true for him. It literally became a self-fulfilling prophecy.

We also need to keep true to our vision of what we want for ourselves, so that we don't succumb to the thinking of others, who believe they know what is best for us. Even though no one can change our thinking but ourselves, we want to consciously keep focused on our desires, or we begin to imagine what others tell us is true. Also, keep in mind that our friends or families do not have to believe the same way we do in order for us to fulfill our desires.

When you begin this practice, there may be a certain lapse of time before you experience what you want. As you become more proficient in imagining your desires fulfilled, you will shorten your time of waiting and will begin to spontaneously experience your dreams come true.

A friend who was having difficulty paying her bills called me up one day and told me she just didn't know how she was going to make it anymore. Being a single mother of two small children, she wanted the flexibility of working for herself, and earning at least enough money to take care of her family. Even though she had a college degree, she just couldn't seem to find a rewarding career. I told her to begin imagining herself already in the perfect working conditions, and also imagining that she had more money then her existing debt. I told her to continue seeing herself this way, despite creditors calling her every day for their money. At first she hesitated, and told me she had tried this way of thinking; she had used affirmations, lit candles, made offerings to the wealth goddesses, and so on. I assured her that she had not persistently done what I suggested, which was to imagine seeing herself *from* her desired state. After I asked her, "What do you have to lose?" she agreed to try using her imagination, and within five weeks she received a telephone call. A gentleman on the other end asked for her, and she almost hung up on him thinking it was another creditor, however an inner feeling prompted her to continue listening to what he had to say. He had been trying to contact her for several years, as she was an heir to a considerable sum of money. Her stepfather who had passed away several years before, had in his younger years started a savings account that apparently no one in the family had been aware of. She not only received $26,000.00, but she now understands how she was kept from receiving the universe's gifts by imagining that she was poor. She started a small business with the money she received, and is now able to take care of her family while working at something she loves.

"The human spirit is so great a thing that no man can express it;
could we rightly comprehend the mind of man,
nothing would be impossible to us upon the earth."
–Paracelsus

By the use of a full, and powerful imagination anything can be created, and only *you* possess the power to create your own reality. Your imagination is a priceless gift, so use it consciously.

Great thinkers throughout history have claimed that through the conscious mind, we could shape events and control matter; the more we begin to study this philosophy, we begin to catch a glimpse of the amazing power of our own mind. Imagination or visualization is the primary power in developing the magnetic forces of the creative mind. *How* the creative mind arranges events to come into existence shouldn't concern us.

Fortunately many of the fears that we entertain in our imagination do not become a reality. If we hold the event temporarily, or for a small amount of time the creative mind doesn't produce that particular event. However, the creative mind can only give you what you imagine passionately for yourself. If the image is dull, scattered or vague, then the outcome will be that as well; doubts, fears and worry also have a part in counteracting what you want. Your happiness, wealth, or success, in fact your entire reality is caused by your imagination. This doesn't imply that you are to become so paranoid if you imagine something you don't want to experience; the simple fact that you are consciously aware of your thoughts will allow you to make the changes that you need.

How can we go about supporting our imagination? The most effective way of influencing the creative mind is through pictures. Having a picture of what you want, directs the conscious mind by giving it feedback of the events you desire in your life. Those who have well-developed imaginations, or use clear pictures possess the ability to create the events they want much faster. You can assist your imagination with a dream book, photographs, affirmations, or quotes, anything that can serve as a constant reminder. Leave out any guess work, and bring in the *magic* by consciously using your imagination.

To become the person you would like to be, imagine yourself doing or having what you want in your life. You can't bring about that million dollars, luxury car or mansion by undirected wishful thinking. Wishful thinking just doesn't have the power to bring about fulfillment of your desires, because you are affirming that what you want is not a reality, so it will be continually held in the future. Your imagination needs to be consciously focused, so that it can gather power to produce the desired end. Whether or not you realize it, you have imagined your present reality, but this does not mean you are powerless to change it. The reality as you know it, has merely been what you expected to see, and is a picture of your expectations. From the time you were a small child you accepted many things you were told as being genuine even though they were not. You accepted them as the ultimate truth, in effect you convinced yourself that what you were told, was the truth. All you have to do now, is to consciously do the same thing with your imagination. This works, simply because the creative mind cannot distinguish between what is true, false, great or small.

It may seem that certain experiences were thrust upon us when we were growing up, so we can never be successful because we come from a family of losers. We feel we are not educated enough, intelligent enough or simply do not have the qualities it takes to make it. We sabotage ourselves with this type of thinking but events in our lives can be changed for the better, however this takes a certain amount of effort along with determination. We are constantly molding our lives by our imagination, and our outer experiences have been matched up to our inner imagination with great precision. To have a life filled with true abundance, you have to create a new self-image, and feel that you do have the qualities it takes to have anything you want.

Even as you are faced with a challenge, don't give it so much importance that it traumatizes you. The more you consciously use the power of your imagination, the more powerful it becomes. This journey may be challenging at first, so this is the very time you need to focus your attention, and not give up. Also, remember there is a solution within every problem.

The initial time that you spend working with your imagination is the most important; in the beginning there tends to be a cleansing process to clear the mind of the accumulation of all the thoughts, and beliefs that no longer serve you. These beliefs are under your control, and as you begin to integrate this material, you will know exactly how you created your own reality, and how you can change it. You will learn how to recognize those limiting beliefs, how to manage them, and how they have caused your reality. This has all been created because of what you have imagined as being true for yourself!

Feature Article

We have the power to be anything we desire, if we just use our imagination consciously. What we imagine for our future, also influences the decisions we make right now.

Just imagine that you have achieved your dream, and now a well-known publication wants to write a feature article about you.

Pretend that you are the editor of the publication; use your imagination creatively to write an exciting and fascinating article about yourself. Use your name throughout the entire article as you explain your contributions and achievements.

Also, determine what type of an award you will receive and what type of publication the article will appear in.

When the article is finished, write an intriguing headline that will capture the attention of readers all over the world; add a creative caption to enhance the pictures or graphics that supplement the article.

Well-known Publication _____

_____

Intriguing Headline _____

_____

Fascinating Article_____

_____

_____

_____

_____

_____

_____

_____

Awards & Honors Received_____

_____

_____

Creative Caption for Pictures & Graphics_____

_____

_____

IT'S IN THE CARDS!

This technique is an excellent way to focus your attention on creating your future from the present moment. Take several 3 x 5 cards, and write down your desires.

Place the cards on your refrigerator door, the bathroom mirror, the dash of your car, your desk or wherever you will see the cards frequently. You want to constantly impress your creative mind with what you desire.

Be sure to state what you want as existing in the present. Statements of I AM are very powerful and very important. The individual is a part of the Universal I AM. The I AM consciousness refers to that part of thought which is both conscious and creative, and it not only aligns you with your affirmation but also with Universal Consciousness.

If you think your affirmations contradict your present circumstances, please keep in mind that you are now consciously creating what you want. I AM has resounded throughout the ages and has created a tremendous path of energy which unites us with the impersonal Universal Consciousness. Everything in nature is united at the most primordial level and there is only one I in the Universe, which is the essence of everything in existence. We can then understand that the Universal I is expressed in many ways. Before every affirmation, align yourself with Universal Consciousness by stating "I AM one with_____."

       (your desire)

Picture This . . .

I AM ONE WITH _____!

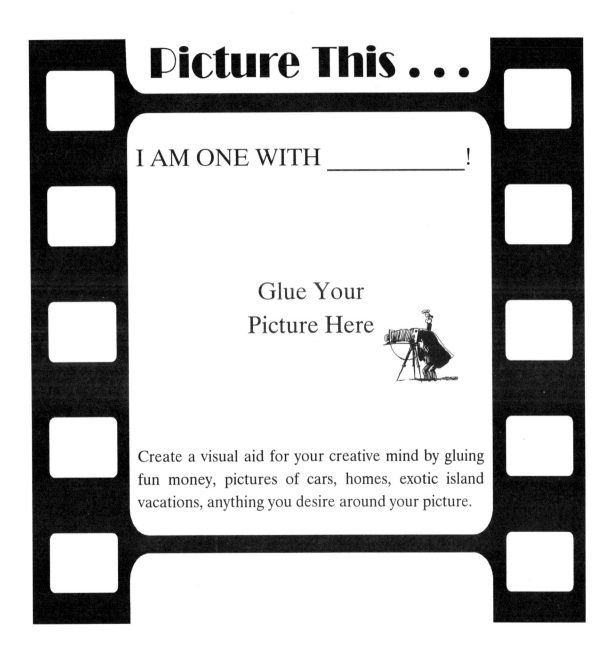

Glue Your
Picture Here

Create a visual aid for your creative mind by gluing fun money, pictures of cars, homes, exotic island vacations, anything you desire around your picture.

2

Think
About
It!

"Our life is what our thoughts make it."
–Marcus Aurelius

Everything we have in our life right now depends solely on the power of our thoughts. Our thoughts have creative power, so choose your thoughts wisely because whatever energy you send out, you receive as well. You can create *magic* with your thoughts!

Most people do not understand the tremendous power thought has – it is a very subtle force that can be used either for your good or your demise. If you continually have negative thoughts about your health, relationships or wealth, you will eventually create some adverse experience in your life. Be aware of those thoughts, feel the energy surrounding them, as this is enough to release them. Don't worry if you do have negative thoughts, however if you are making a habit of negative thinking then you are not consciously using your mind. To control one's thinking means controlling one's destiny. Whether you are conscious or not of your thoughts, you are constantly creating what you have in your life. The mirror of your thoughts is the cause and effect that you experience in your reality. You embody your mental equivalent, so what you accept in your mind as true for yourself, will become true in your experiences. To transcend karma is to use the mind consciously!

We may not imagine certain things are going to happen to us, but certain types of thought will produce certain conclusions in our life. This shows us how we want to consciously choose what we imagine or think. Also, we want to be aware of the type of emotion we attach to our thoughts. It is impossible to create something in our imagination without it causing some action. The deeper the emotion (energy in motion), in association with our thought, the greater and more complete the action. If we would become as emotionally charged with our likes as we are with our dislikes, we would manifest our desires more rapidly.

Thoughts work in a similar manner, as dropping a pebble into a pond. The pebble creates a ripple or disturbance in the calm water that continues to move to the outer edges of the pond. Once the ripple touches the outer edge, it traces a path backward to the original spot where the pebble first entered the water. In the same way thoughts create ripples in consciousness, which in turn gives you what you have thought about most. Your conscious thoughts tell a lot about you, i.e., the type of experiences or challenges you will encounter. So, if you consciously observe your thoughts, this will show you the state of your creative mind. This will also show you where you are headed; how and what you are creating through your intentions and desires. Your thoughts will show you very clearly what your future will be. Whatever exists as a physical event had its beginning first in consciousness. This is so important to remember and to consciously be aware of!

Your conscious mind gauges your present situation through your thoughts and feelings, so if you don't like what you are experiencing then consciously change them. By using your conscious mind, and it's cognitive power creatively, you can change the type of message you are sending to your family, friends and even to yourself! If you have feelings of low self-esteem, inferiority or worthlessness, consciously trace backward in time and work on discovering the reasons for these negative emotions and beliefs. You do not want to candy coat your feelings, but confront your feelings of inadequacy and then consciously replace them with empowering thoughts!

The creative mind is sensitive and neutral; it can only give us what we consciously or unconsciously choose. It acts upon thought and as it is neutral, it will not deny the individual, rather it will create what the individual thinks. We imprint upon the creative mind what we think is true about ourselves, and it in return reflects back to us what we think. If we think about poverty and lack then we will project that into our experience – limitation is only the ignorant use of the law of imagination. If we think on abundance then abundance will be the out-picturing of our consciousness.

We sleep collectively and until we wake up, we live by the social conditioning that prevails for the majority of people, and the majority has believed in lack. The prophet tells us what to expect based upon the collective consciousness of a sleeping humanity, and it is true that most individuals live their lives distracted, much like sleepwalkers. They are as if in a dream; they aren't consciously aware of their thoughts, feelings or beliefs and they wonder why certain experiences are happening to them. Many people are so filled with fear that they become paralyzed, and are unable to live their lives to the fullest potential. We *can* wake up individually, understand that we create our own reality, that we are the center of our own universe (which is a most freeing concept) and know that we can make changes in every aspect of our lives.

Directing the creative mind with a centered thought is greater then any specific use of the law of cause and effect. Whether you think of one dollar or millions of dollars, it doesn't matter to the creative mind because it doesn't discriminate between positive, negative, size or quantity, unlike the conscious mind, it doesn't reason or analyze. If it did, it would never accept the self-defeating thinking many people continue do. It doesn't stop to ask if a belief is good or bad, or if an idea is right for a person. It just accepts whatever you imprint upon it, and your creative mind can lead you to failure, as well as success. Remember, if you wish for something, you keep it in the future, therefore consciously focus on what you want, think *from* it and feel as though it is complete.

There is no need to force or coerce your creative mind, just consciously focus on your desires. Thought is the starting point of every new creation, so it should be conscious thought. Think with clarity and imagine only that which you want to bring into existence. Directed thought is infinitely more powerful then undirected thought, and since thought is the bridge between your creative mind and your reality, doesn't it make sense to spend time being aware of your thoughts? Directed thought acts much like a laser, because it is focused and concentrated, making it more precise and powerful in producing what you experience. The concentration and intensity of focused thought cuts right through all the obstacles you have previously created with your thinking, and this allows your message to go directly to the creative mind. Undirected thought is much the same as regular light, its energy is diffused and it just doesn't have the intensity of a concentrated beam of light.

What do you choose? A life filled with abundance and riches, or a status quo existence? Our outer world is merely a reflection of our thinking, so we cannot achieve our goals or change the world without transforming ourselves first. As within, so without. Hold fast to your dream and nothing can stop you from creating it!

The essence of thought is desire and desire is the creative force urging you to express more of life, which in turn creates action. The subtle law of thought does exist and you receive precisely what you think about most. This is a thinking universe, and whether or not you are aware of it, doesn't change this truth. Every time we think, we set the creative law into motion, so put your attention on what you want. The world and everyone you meet reflect what you think you deserve; life truly is a 360-degree mirror and is constantly reflecting the mirror image of your inner thinking. Your intuition is merely your creative mind reflecting back to you what you have really desired in your life, and it is trying to attract your attention to lead you into action.

I have a friend that believes life is a constant struggle, and most everyone he meets gives him a difficult time; they are mirroring his belief in struggle. In reality he is creating his own life drama, because he just doesn't believe that he deserves to receive anything, unless it is difficult to come by. He also believes that everyone is always out to take something from him. He is a tailor and one day he went into work early to tailor a suit for a customer, who needed it in a rush. My friend took the extra time to have the suit ready, and when his customer came in, he said he forgot his checkbook but would mail a check out when he got home. My friend's intuition caused him to hesitate but he gave his customer the suit anyway. After two weeks of not receiving payment, my friend called asking when he might receive a check. His customer told him he wasn't going to pay him, because he didn't like the tailoring work. My friend suggested he bring the suit back, and he would fix whatever needed to be done. His customer said, "Just forget it, I don't have time to bring it in"! Needless to say, my friend gave away his power by not listening to his intuition, or honoring himself by allowing his customer to walk out of the shop without paying. This whole episode merely reinforced his thinking that life is a struggle. Too many individuals think their thoughts and moods are effects, and not causes of their experience. Moods are not only the result of what is happening in our lives, but are also the *causes*. It is done unto you as you believe!

Let's set the groundwork to break those habits that no longer serve you, establish new attitudes and behaviors for fulfillment, happiness and wealth. You can begin by changing your reality through the use of relaxation, affirmation, visualization and meditation. A relaxed state allows you to subdue your conscious mind, and directly contact the creative mind. This puts you in control and now you can introduce what you want to create in your life, without your conscious mind challenging it. Affirmations are simple positive statements and it is important to state affirmations in the present, or the creative mind will think there is no hurry in what you want. Affirm with emotion, give the affirmation impact! Some people are great at visualization, while others hear or feel concepts, so work with a method that seems most comfortable to you. Just know that there is tremendous power in your thoughts and words, and when they are in alignment, you will create synchronicity in your life. Be aware of your thoughts of lack and poverty, feel your emotions to release them, then replace them with thoughts of wealth, prosperity and happiness.

> "The ancestor to every action is thought."
> –Ralph Waldo Emerson

Everyone who is successful has either consciously or unconsciously made use of the power of thought and imagination. In fact, everything we have in our possession has come about as a result of our creative thinking. It is not a question of whether we use our imagination, but *how* we use our imagination. When you think about meeting a friend for lunch, you first imagine where you will meet, how you will get there and you even imagine what you will wear. The thoughts may be very quick and fleeting, but you first create future events in your imagination, nonetheless. All great fortunes, great discoveries, inventions, the advancement of technology, and in fact, all achievement originated first in thought. The secret of success lies within the thoughts of individuals, not without. With this we begin to comprehend that our world is governed by thought and everything without had its counterpart originally within consciousness.

Your life, which includes your experiences, challenges, professional and social status, and even your character, is determined by your thoughts. By this, I think you can better understand the statement, "Thoughts can either make or break a person". Therefore, there can be no action either positive or negative, without the generating force of thought behind it.

> "There is nothing either good or bad,
> but thinking makes it so."
> –Shakespear

Thoughts and ideas have an electromagnetic quality, and when combined with the intensity of your beliefs, the creative mind begins organizing those concepts. You are then directed to those areas where you can experience your desires with others of like mind. Your thoughts literally draw those to you who wish to participate in a similar experience as you. You telepathically send out information as well as receive it, and you can only receive information which you are psychically tuned into. There is a constant exchange of ideas and thoughts between yourself and others both on a telepathic, as well as conscious level. Collectively at very subtle levels of consciousness we do share a general agreement, so that we perceive our environment in much the same way. You are given the gift of creating your reality and knowing this, gives you the great secret of freedom to experience what humanity perceives as miracles.

When we are *not* consciously thinking, we are many times greatly influenced by the thoughts of others, newspapers, television, books or even by remarks from bystanders, and if we allow these thoughts to influence our creative mind, they can become a directive force. The conscious mind is meant to decipher what we take in from our environment, and to make clear assumptions about what is right for us. Most of the things we hear and witness are not of a positive or enriching nature, therefore we want to consciously determine what is important to us, and filter out those thoughts that do not result in pure fulfillment. When there is a fully developed thought and when the creative mind has clarity of what we want, our desires will be translated as our reality. Our failures or successes are caused more by what *we* think, rather than by our abilities or expertise.

> "All that we are is the result of what we have thought."
> –Buddha

What may appear as a coincidence is not a coincidence at all; it is the outcome of your thoughts. Whatever the character of your thought, whatever you steadily focus upon, is what you will attract into your life. If you really want change, then you have to determinedly take time each day to examine those beliefs that come to you, and decide whether they present a false picture of what you want or if they fit with your ideals. If those ideas and beliefs don't fit with your picture of reality, discard them and consciously affirm what you do want. The creative mind will go into action to create what you want; it will find the way to overcome any obstacle or challenge for you. Trust that your thoughts are creative and use your conscious mind properly.

Science will gradually accept that this invisible force of thought exists, as more individuals begin using the secrets in this book. The law of thought is as natural as any other force in nature, so there is no need to be superstitious about it, rather treat it and accept it as you do gravity, electricity or electromagnetic energy. Thoughts are highly concentrated energy carrying electromagnetically coded information to the creative mind, which begins the organizational patterns to create your physical reality. When you emphasize or focus on positive thoughts, they become highly "charged" with energy, and this applies to your negative thoughts as well. Whatever you firmly believe, and whatever you focus your attention on, you literally "charge" with energy and information to draw the thing to you. If someone were to say something negative to you, don't give it so much attention, just let it pass by you and understand that it is their "stuff" not yours!

"Miracles happen, not in opposition to Nature,
but in opposition to what we know of Nature."
–St. Augustine

How you think, feel and live will depend upon your own individual blueprint. You are not only an individual expression of Universal Consciousness, but you are the architect in your life and you cannot have exactly the same experience as another. You design your life, you draw up the plans and you decide what you want! What is true for one person does not mean it is true for another. You assume that you must be on guard, because of what you see on the news station, or hear on the radio of perilous events; you believe the incidents could also happen to you. In fact, our news media convinces you that you must be aware of every event that is happening outside of you, and to be prepared for the inevitable disaster of a stock market crash, recession, accident, burglary; it goes on ad infinitum. You do experience whatever you concentrate upon, and this is an absolute truth. Each and every one of us is unique, we all have different experiences and we can play out an infinite number of dramas and situations, in fact, there is no limit to what we can experience. But we choose, we are the creators of our reality and depending on what we think, we either create a life of wealth and happiness, or a life of hardship. Change your thinking and the existing circumstances in your life will disappear, because whatever you give your energy to, will flourish and whatever you take your energy away from, will wither and die. You will however, walk through whatever you set into motion, so consciously be aware of your thinking. Invest in yourself and focus your attention upon what you want. Look at what you have created for yourself up to this moment, examine the contents of your mind because you react to what you believe, not only consciously but subconsciously.

Remember, humanity dominates the ordinary existence and thinks that life is reflected by the winds of fate, when in fact each and every one of us is creating our reality directly, so break away and experience the extraordinary!

Feel Free to Express Yourself!

This exercise creates a very powerful way to open your awareness concerning the ideas, beliefs and thoughts you hold about yourself. There is no right, wrong or special way of completing this exercise.

Just be open to the experience of feeling your emotions, as they begin to surface. There are no time limitations or experiences that you should have. Accept what you feel, and know that what happens, is your unique way of getting in touch with yourself. If you become irritated, upset or nervous, feel those emotions, because all they want is to be expressed and when they are, you will find that you become more centered.

1.   Close your eyes and take a few deep breaths.

2.   Sense any emotions deep inside you and allow them to come up. Do not judge the feelings, but merely experience them. (There could be a whole range of emotions). When you allow your emotions to be expressed, you won't be so overwhelmed by them, and this will allow you to return to more creative thinking.

3.   Write down some of the beliefs and feelings that you had during this exercise. These are energies that you are carrying with you all the time that are influencing how you experience your reality.

4.   Close your eyes again and see a thread attached to each one of the energies individually. Follow the thread back to where that energy was first formed. This will give you a glimpse of how long you have had these feelings. Now you can determine whether or not you wish to continue sustaining them in your life.

NOW THAT'S SYNCHRONICITY!

For the next week be aware of spontaneous occurrences that take place in your life.

Write all of these down on paper; this will show you that synchronicity happens all the time.

Now, write down any meaningful events that took place during the week. These are not necessarily spontaneous; rather they have great meaning to you. Think back to a time before the event took place. Did you think or want something such as this to happen?

NOW, THAT'S SYNCHRONICITY!_____

_____

_____

_____

NOW, THAT'S MEANINGFUL!_____

_____

_____

_____

3

Surrender
To
The
Universe!

"You need not leave your room.
Remain sitting at your table and listen.
You need not even listen, simply wait.
You need not even wait, just learn to become quiet,
and still and solitary.
The world will freely offer itself to you to be unmasked.
It has no choice, it will roll in ecstasy at your feet."
–Franz Kafka

Many people believe the statement, "Let the universe handle the details", implies that they don't have to make choices, or think about what they want in life when in fact, nothing could be further from the truth! It means that you must first choose what you want, without concerning yourself about *how* it will take place. Leave the details to your creative mind, as it has its own way of making contacts and of opening avenues that you may never have even thought of. Simply continue to keep what you want active in your awareness – that's all.

You could receive support from the most unexpected sources, so don't block your good by intellectualizing how the events will work themselves out. You might miss important clues! You will find that clues will come at the most unexpected times too! You may suddenly have a compelling idea or thought to call someone you have never seen before, or you may even hear from a long lost friend. Pay attention to those thoughts and events that seem out of the ordinary and follow your intuition, as this is the way you make those valuable connections.

Successful individuals have achieved wealth, power and fame, made tremendous accomplishments, overcome great challenges, as well as cured physical problems by impressing upon the creative mind what they wanted. The creative mind's power is there for you to use, and the only step you have to take, is to believe in it's power.

The creative mind is connected to the source of all power – it holds the wisdom of the past – the awareness and knowing of the present moment – the vision of the future, and it lies within each and every one of us. The ancients called the creative mind the "Spirit or Self", while others have referred to this intelligence or consciousness, as the super-ego – the super-conscious – the unconscious – the small still voice, etc. In any event, we are linked with this Universal Consciousness, which is the source of energy, intelligence, creativity and infinite organizing power displayed within every living and inanimate thing in existence. It is the essence of life, and it's powers are limitless. It never sleeps, it warns of impending danger, and guides us to action in what we may perceive as miracles; it is the most formidable force in shaping and controlling our lives.

It not only is the source of power for all of us and our actions; it is the source of all our thoughts. The discovery is that Universal Consciousness interacts with itself to produce creation, and our essential being is part of it. When we align with this deepest level of life then we can have whatever we put our attention on.

Life is played on the playing field of Universal Consciousness, and the purpose of our life is for it to be expressed. Awareness is having inward knowledge and being mentally awake to the natural laws, which give us the important secrets to achieve our goals and realize our dreams. We have been unaware of the connection between Universal Consciousness and ourselves, and that we possess the power to create wealth, poverty, tragedy or magic in our lives.

Intuition, bursts of inspiration, creativity, knowing, bliss, dynamism and imagination are all the higher functions of the creative mind. It performs most successfully when we plant the seeds of our desires just after we have taken time to quiet our conscious mind.

Whether you want to make money, be successful in business, have loving relationships or be the best in whatever you endeavor, the creative mind perceives, and it works where you apply and listen to it. Allow your creative mind to handle the details, so that your life becomes joyful and carefree!

The simple act of deciding begins to create your reality. If you think you are powerless to change things and go along with this type of thinking, you are choosing this. If you decide you want to experience something else, you choose that. Decision is your intent to experience certain events in your life, you have a wealth of experiences to choose from and you can decide what you want.

Levels of Consciousness

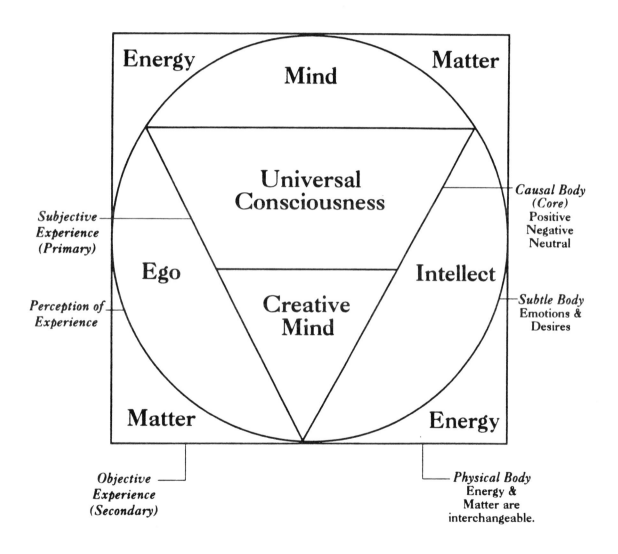

4

Open
Sesame!

"I am the beginning and the end,
there is nothing to come that has not been and is."
–Ecclesiastes 3:15

Thermodynamics has given us knowledge that energy and matter are interchangeable. Quantum physics states that no energy is ever lost; rather it is transformed and takes on a different quality while the chief substance essentially remains the same. This theory applies to us, as well as to everything else in the universe.

All realities and dramas exist as probabilities; when we use our imagination and thought, we tap into them. The universe is just one big cosmic play; the script and all the roles already exist. There are an infinite number of roles available to be acted out; we can even decide which scripts and roles we want to play. The extraordinary thing however, is that the producer is flexible, so we can change the roles we play at anytime. Shh! Quiet! The stage has been set and here come the players.

"All the world's a stage and all the
men and women merely players."
–Shakespeare

It has been described many times that we live in a holographic universe, which means that all probabilities exist *within* us. As with a hologram, the part (us) carries information of the whole (Universal Consciousness). Through our imagination and attention, we activate the holographic template (which contains infinite treasures), and gives us what we imagine ourselves to be. There are all kinds of treasures just waiting to be discovered by you, and the state of your consciousness is your demand on the infinite treasure-house; it gives Universal Consciousness the order to create your supply. You only have to change your attention and your state of consciousness, to change the supply. Infinite probabilities also exist outside of space and time, therefore you must first direct your attention toward what you want, to bring it into existence. Our thoughts create the energy, to impact the holographic template of infinite probabilities. Then those probabilities materialize to become a physical reality or space time event. You literally choose the type of world you will live in by your thoughts, so with this knowledge it is important to be aware of what you are choosing. Your world is literally an expression of your consciousness and for this reason, it is very important that you live in the present moment, and be consciously aware of your thoughts. Universal Consciousness contains everything; be it positive, negative or neutral and what you impress upon it, is exactly what you will experience.

> "The past is history
> The future is a mystery
> Today is a gift
> That is why it is called the present."
> –Anonymous

If you are continually thinking about the past, you are reinforcing it and you are continuing to keep it in the present. Even, if the same people are not involved in your life that were in your past, others will participate in your present to continue your past drama. You can turn your life around by acknowledging that the point of power is in the present moment, and that you have created everything you have in your life right now. Each moment actually houses an event which is dictated by what you think. If you continually live in the future, and I often find people doing what I call failure forecasting, then you are literally choosing that for your next experience.

Let's say you look at your checkbook and you are low on money. You start playing intellectual volleyball in your mind, you think back and forth about how you're going to pay the rent, pay the car payment and pay the bills that are stacking up. Now, you begin your great circus act, so you juggle here and juggle there trying to find the money to pay your bills. You think about how you can cut back on one end, how you can borrow money from your parents and friends, or how you can pay a small amount here and there to hold you over. You begin to create this plan of action and you hope, hope, hope that everything will work out, and even though you have only been working on what your next step is for the last half hour, you drop into your chair exhausted! Now, look at what you have been imagining for yourself; look at all the energy you have expended, and you are no further along then you were a half hour ago. You are learning the hard way how your thoughts create your reality, and just how consistently they create. Your thoughts have just imprinted upon your creative mind to begin creating events by what you have imagined. Why can't you stop this eternal chatter in your mind and let the creative mind handle the details? Why are you always assuming the worst possible scenario for yourself, instead of something great to become your experience? It is because you have exercised your mind to always believe the worst, so you must now consciously exercise your creative mind to bring about a shift in your thinking, and you will see wealth materialize as if by magic!

Consciousness is the only eternal reality; it is the primary source of creation. Absolutely nothing outside of you creates the circumstances you presently find yourself in, so why do you keep coming to certain conclusions for yourself? Your senses tell you that your desires are impossible and through habit you accept this as true. All you need to do, is to consciously impress your creative mind that you already possess your desires. Remember, your so-called rational thinking keeps you stuck by what you see as concrete and convinces you that change is impossible. You truly need to stop listening to others about the logical way of living; start right now to create an effortless and fulfilling way to live. Our experiences are simply created by what we expect to see. Our brains are the instruments that we use to translate the information we receive from the universe we live in, so how we perceive the world is manufactured in the brain. We seem to always look at external things to justify our present situation when in fact, we need to look within. We begin to set up our future based upon what we think are the facts and how we feel about past events.

Universal Consciousness constantly supports us and we can trust it. We can either view the world as a safe place or a dangerous place, but whatever we decide, that is the possibility we give energy to, which in turn determines our reality. Attention on what we want creates the experiences that we will have; it activates the holographic template. Nothing becomes concrete in our lives until we think it, imagine it and feel it. Our struggles come about because we simply cannot imagine that the possibility exists, for us to have what we want. This moment right now, is the height of your power, so use it wisely for the best possible outcome.

"He who lives in the present lives in eternity."
–Ludwig Wittgenstein

Now, if you really understand Universal Consciousness, then you'll understand that time is just a construct of our conscious mind, and that linear time does not really exist in the larger sense. Now, before you think this is too abstract, let me coach you on this. Right now, think about time. Does the past exist? No. Does the future exist? No. Then the only time that exists is the present. Our memories keep the past alive, and we have to use our imagination to think about the future, therefore the only moment that exists, is this moment right now! Our ancient scholars and enlightened sages knew that the point of power was in the present. What we experience is nothing other then a set of events that we perceive as time; knowing this allows us to change events, through what we are thinking right now. You are consistently impressing the field of infinite probabilities; a treasure of events just waiting for you to experience.

You can become a successful conscious creator and you can literally change your life, if you just focus your mind on thoughts that bring you a quality lifestyle. Many sages have presented the following secret, but it really took me awhile to understand it, rather than just intellectualizing it. "You create your own reality and your point of power is in the present moment." Every day I repeat this simple statement to bring it to my awareness, to keep focused in the present, and to know the truth of how I am constantly creating. Also, by repeating this, you are conditioning the creative mind through the wonderful process of self-suggestion.

> "To conquer fear is the beginning of wisdom."
> –Bertrand Russell

Our thoughts of fear are just as creative as positive thoughts in attracting results, therefore no matter what the character of the thought, it does create after its kind. Fear is based only on your feelings and emotions related to some past experience. You tend to believe these experiences will continue when in fact, it is your imagination and thinking that is keeping them alive. Since fear is based only on your memory and how you felt about a certain experience, it continues to be a part of your reality, because you give it energy by your thinking. A good friend suggested that I consider fear this way – "F E A R – False Evidence Appearing Real". When you are continually in fear, you generate the energy needed, to eventually bring whatever you fear into your experience; this also continues to reinforce your thinking. If you become afraid of negative emotions or thoughts, you tend to repress them, so the best action to take, is to create new feelings and emotions around what you want. You may think that negative thoughts have a tremendous power over you when in fact, it is your *belief* that gives them power, your belief literally "charges" your thoughts.

The ensuing secret is very powerful to know; never act or make important decisions when you are in fear, hurried, frustrated, angry, undecided or in a negative state of consciousness. If any of these emotions occur during a time when you feel a decision must be made, the decision can wait until you have time to center yourself. Never, ever make a decision based on fear! This is not referring to the times, when you are *spontaneously* motivated to take action.

You can clear your mind in the present moment, and know that this is where all of creation begins and ends. Living in the present moment stops the anxiety of the future and the fear from the past; you can break the hold that fear has on you, but this takes a person willing to work at it. Just face your fears, then replace them with new thought!

Instead of saying that wealth is not for you or that you never have enough money, consciously make a decision that you will condition your creative mind. Begin by stating, the only time that exists is this moment; you are perfectly fine right now, and you do create your future with the thoughts you are currently entertaining now. Continue to focus on positive statements, then when a negative thought comes up give it attention, and allow it to move through you to be released. You can resolve and create a solution just by taking your attention away from what you perceive, as a non-negotiable problem. Trust that everything will work out, and that you do have the power to create your reality.

It really isn't difficult to break the cycle of fear if you understand that everything in existence, is consciousness. All you really have to do is change what you believe to be true and replace it with something that you want, even though you can't see it right now. You want the ability to live life effortlessly and with a sense of power to live each moment with passion. Even though this knowledge may be new for you, you can integrate it, and feel the freedom by knowing that you are the only one who creates your reality.

Our reality isn't based upon events that are consecutive but rather on events that we perceive to be consecutive. By this, we can better understand how we can alter the past, and how we create our future experience. Living in the present moment releases you from having to work out details, and allows you to release those things from the past that no longer serve you. Work on living in the now! If you think you can conceal your thoughts, think again because what you hold in your consciousness will be exactly what you experience. Even words cannot hide your actions. Your reality is always a reflection of your state of mind, and the people you meet will show you who you are by *their* behavior. Therefore, stop trying to change the world and others, since they are only acting as your mirror, magnifying your state of consciousness. It is like breaking a mirror hoping to change your face when it is only reflecting *who you are.* What you believe about yourself should be the most important thing in this world to you. You must live in the consciousness of your ideal, thereby allowing

Universal Consciousness to support you and set you free. If you are confident in your mind then there will be nothing to contradict that. You may think you are fooling others, but you cannot fool consciousness, as it builds your next experience based upon your thinking. Most importantly, take a higher thought surrounding your experiences, and understand that you walk through what you project into consciousness. Even if you think you have substantial data that suggests events will turn out a certain way, just impress your conscious mind with the thoughts of what you want, which in turn will impress your creative mind. You will be greatly surprised at the outcome of your future. Events can be changed, but most people go along with what they think seems to be so final, rather then use their imagination, and the power of the present moment to create a change.

When you put your attention on your intention, you create the blueprint for the makings of your reality. It is as though you are the architect in your life and your thoughts are the blueprints that set the plans for your experiences. All you have to do is change your thought, and you change your reality. For instance, what would happen if an architect used the same blueprints of an already existing building to build another one? It would look exactly like the first building, so if the architect wanted to have a different building then he would have to change the blueprint; that's all you have to do with your imagination and thoughts.

The following is a very insightful discovery; each of us is the center of our own universe, and only we can live in our own individual reality. Now, we can share a certain reality and experience similar events, but we still will not experience the exact same reality, because our experiences are unique to us only. Since each of our lives is played out in its own exceptional way, we cannot take anything away from someone else. We don't even have to compete with another for what we perceive as the same event – so everyone wins! Now, suppose you want a particular event to take place in your life, all you have to do, is close your eyes and imagine what you want it to be. You are impressing your creative mind with your thoughts, which actually creates a disturbance in consciousness. Continue to use your imagination every day until what you want has become a reality. It may be starting your own business, buying a new car or receiving money.

You encounter an event in consciousness before you encounter it as an experience; all events that occur in the physical dimension were first formed in consciousness. There is so much more to you, then you can see physically, in fact your greater dimensional being is, Universal Consciousness. When you connect with this greater aspect of yourself, you do not have to create any effort around what you want in this physical dimension.

One very important thing to remember, there is no reason for you to act through or depend directly on others to get what you want. You do not need money, family or friends, the right timing or influence to fulfill your dreams. All you have to do is imagine what you want. Your creative mind will support your decision by sending others to you who will help you, or by giving you directions through your intuition who to contact.

Do not look to see if your imaginal act is really going to harden into fact, simply know that it is already complete. Keep your mood light, and the "universe will come rolling at your feet". If you are continually looking outside of your consciousness for answers, or to the causes of why you are experiencing the reality you are in now, then you are not convinced of it's power. You will always find what you seek; excuses for your setbacks, excuses why something won't work, or excuses to justify your helplessness. You have no one to change but yourself in order to experience a magical life.

Our ancient teachers knew we could alter our future, our reality, and our experiences just by changing our consciousness; this information has always been available to us. You have the power to alter your future or the past, because consciousness is open ended, in fact it acts much like plastic, whatever thought you impress upon it that is what is created. Although you have prepared a certain outcome for your future with your thoughts, the good news is that if you want to change your future, there are an infinite number of possibilities and futures to choose from, just by using your imagination. The past and the future are purely imaginal, but in a wider sense they are part of the present. Our waking state is directed by our senses, and our imagined state is directed by our desires. In our imagination we see what we want to see, and when we consciously do this, we create what the world will see.

When you engage your creative mind, you are actually connecting with Universal Consciousness and invoking its guidance. There really is no separation between the creative mind and Universal Consciousness; the creative mind *is* the individual expression of the whole. Consciousness is the one and only presence. It pervades everything; in the world of imagination we use it to create; in the world of sense we use it to see and experience.

Your imagination is of great value, because it opens the doors to the infinite probabilities that you can experience. If you are experiencing poverty, you have attracted that probability, because you have chosen that for your experience. But the probability still exists for prosperity, and with a shift in your thinking, you can access that reality.

Put It To The Carbon Test

The following technique is an ancient custom. It is thought that by burning an item, the essence of it is transferred to wherever you want it to go.

Think about the changes you want to make in your life: acquiring more wealth, establishing enriching relationships, breaking negative bonds or old patterns with others, anything you want changed. Now, write a letter listing all the things you want with a carbon-based pencil; this allows your stored electromagnetic energy to be transferred through the pencil. Drop the letter into the fireplace, and allow the letter to burn completely, so it carries the essence of what you wrote into the ethers.

This exercise actually allows you to direct your attention. It is thought that the person you are writing to, will receive your message at the subtle and causal level (emotional, mental and spiritual). You can also write yourself a letter, to get in touch with your subtle and causal bodies.

If you find that you have inherited beliefs from generations past that no longer serve you, then you can break the karmic chain simply by writing a letter. Write down that you no longer will carry this karmic debt financially, spiritually, physically or emotionally and that you are a divine, prosperous, wealthy and loving being.

This statement demands the truth about you and you are claiming your right to be free from any past events.

Expand Your Consciousness

Imagine you could be in several places at one time, anywhere in the world, and in any dimension. This activity is designed to encourage creativity, stimulate your imagination, and expand your consciousness.

Imagine a time in the distant past. What do you see? Who are you with? Where are you?

Now, imagine that you are traveling – travel to any part of the world. What do you see? Who are you with? Where are you?

Now, imagine that you are in another dimension of space and time. What do you see? Who are you with? Where are you?

Write down your experiences, and also note that you transcend the physical just by consciously using your imagination.

Bring your awareness to the present moment, and become aware of your surroundings. Notice if there are any pictures on the wall, furniture or people that may be sharing the same room with you. These surroundings have been there all the time, but you just became conscious of them in this present moment.

Now, continue on, and imagine a future event. Travel to any time, place or dimension that you want. What do you see? Who are you with? Where are you?

This activity is a great way to experience the sensation of your imagination, as it takes your awareness to uncharted territories.

For the next week use your consciousness to begin predicting future events. It doesn't matter if you are correct, or not. Your consciousness will expand into areas that are not familiar to you. If you continue working with this exercise, you will discover that you become more and more aware of future events. Your intuition will begin to work more successfully, and you will begin perceiving information that is highly significant to you.

5

Come
To
Your
Senses!

"Success produces success, just as money produces money."
–Sebastien Chamfort

Your environment is an extension of your thoughts, emotions and beliefs; it is an extension of *you*. Through what you have been taught, and through the trick of your senses you believe that you are separate from it. You interpret your environment through your senses combined with what you expect to see, which is based upon your beliefs and ideas. You perceive physical matter as solid when in fact, quantum physics has proven that matter is 99.9% space and that matter isn't solid at all, rather it is made up of quickly moving particles. This brings us to the truth that everything has a vibratory frequency including thought.

Sight, sound, touch, taste and smell all have a different vibrational frequency. We use our five senses to send coded messages to our brain. The coded messages are actually vibrations, which are sent via our nervous system to be deciphered by us. If we see the color blue, it is the vibration of the color blue gathered by the sense of sight, and then transmitted to the brain. If we hear a loud noise, then that comes to us through the vibration of sound. Our five senses act as an anchor for our memory, so right now, just imagine a holiday or a special day, and what you enjoyed about that day. Think about the aroma of baked goods, the sight of festive decorations, the sound of music, the delicious taste of the food or the laughter and fun you had while sharing the special day with others. The difference in the composition of each vibration, determines how we access our senses.

So, what does this have to do with us? Well, vibrations are how we interpret the world that we have created with our thoughts. Thoughts are actually sounds vibrating in consciousness. You have probably heard the following statement many times, "I can't hear myself think", this is because we hear our thoughts. Our physical reality has not only been formed by our beliefs, but it also reinforces our beliefs.

Now you can use your senses in a way that convinces your creative mind that you can have, what you want. If you want a certain type of automobile, then you might visit a dealership and take a particular car for a drive, absorbing everything about it through all of your senses. In doing this, you consciously impress your creative mind, through the use of your five senses that you want this car. You are also using your five senses to impress upon your conscious mind that this can become your reality. Therefore use your senses consciously to create greater and greater richness in your life, and begin using them to transform your beliefs. Since your reality is the result of your perceptions, and you believe only what your senses tell you (which is very limited), you can alter your perception by introducing new data. This instructs your creative mind to begin transforming your reality.

You created memory by using your senses; now you can use your imagination and how you perceived the car to trigger your memory at any time. The conscious mind uses the five senses as well as your intuition – your sixth sense – to synthesize new patterns, and to stimulate the creative mind. Stimulating the energy of the creative mind helps you to focus energy, while expanding your opportunities.

All of your physical experiences are perceived through your senses and are characterized depending on *who you are*. You experience what you have imagined; your creative mind directs your senses to only perceive what you put your attention on. Your focused attention is concentrated through your beliefs, and you only experience that which you are focused upon. You are constantly transforming your experiences with what you believe to be true. You may not think you are making changes because usually they are so subtle, but changes are taking place nonetheless.

By organizing what you want along definite lines, you give it more energy, and this will emphasize one event over another. Continue to expand your experiences by consciously using your senses. Know that whatever you have in your life is based upon your beliefs, and not upon some concrete condition, which you have no control over.

Every cell in your body has intelligence and also memory. When you use your imagination to activate certain feelings, this also acts as a stimulus to the memory housed in your cells. There is a playback from your cellular memory not only to your creative mind, but also to your conscious mind. Science has shown us the correlation between the mind and the body; the mind being the subjective experience of consciousness, and the body being the objective. If you think of an unhappy thought you can experience the sensation somewhere in your body. If you think of something delightful, then sensations are created in the body related to those thoughts.

Your thoughts and feelings are alive, and they create a great amount of energy within you, even if their makeup isn't as tangible as your body. We've also said that thoughts have an electromagnetic quality, which attract events to you that match up to your thinking. Your imagination and thoughts are also triggered by association. Let's take the word rose, what thoughts or feelings come up for you? You may think of the flower, the color red, and imagine the fragrance, or you may think of your aunt named Rose, who lives in the country raising horses; the association goes on ad infinitum. In this way we can understand how, something so intangible can have such a great effect upon us, even to the point of altering our experiences.

We can use our senses in many ways, one way is to create memory; the other is to access and interpret information. We can use all five of our senses, sight, sound, touch, taste and smell to give us information. We can also use our sixth sense, the intuition, to interpret information and give us feedback, so that a kind of "knowing" is created. We can then act on that "knowing", understanding that we are being directed in the right way to fulfill our desires.

My husband had just finished paying a stack of invoices, so we drove to the post office to mail them. We were also going to stop by a friend of ours, who had asked to borrow $600 for a trip he was taking. When my husband handed me the stack of letters, he didn't tell me the last envelope contained the $600 for our friend. So, when we stopped at the post office, I mailed all the letters in my hand. When we arrived at our friends home, my husband asked me for the envelope with the money in it. I looked at him in surprise and said, "I thought you had the money in your wallet"? He replied that he had just put it in an envelope, and gave it to me with the other envelopes. When the realization dawned on us that I had mailed the envelope with the cash in it, my husband went into a mild form of shock. I started laughing because of the folly of the whole event, but I had a "knowing" we would get the envelope back. It took us thirty minutes to reach the post office, and my husband asked me if I would go in (he was still a bit shaken) to get the post-man to help us. I said teasingly, "Why do think it will be a post-man and not a post-woman"? Well, I went into the post office, asked for help and the fellow I was talking to said, "I'll get the guy who handles this kind of situation to help you". Based on his comment, I thought maybe my intuition wasn't working as keenly as it usually does, because I had felt all along that a woman would be handing me the envelope with our money in it. I waited a few minutes, and you'll be surprised to know that a woman did indeed come out to help me. We walked out to the mailbox, she opened the back of it, retrieved our envelope, and handed it to me all the while laughing too! She was very helpful, and said that this type of thing happens all the time!

If you just become quiet, so that you can hear your inner voice, you will experience a type of "knowing". This will greatly help you in your day to day activities, and when you have "knowing", you can take the right direction in your choices. Insight is just another term for intuition, or the small still voice. What we are really referring to, is the ability to look inside for the answers; to see the wisdom within, and only you have the capability to do that. Many times we look to others for our answers, when we need to just take a few minutes to ask ourselves this question, "What do I need to know about this situation"? Don't try to force an answer, just let it gently come up because the information will be there, and you will experience a complete "knowing".

To accelerate your thoughts, create synchronicity, knowing, and to stimulate the creative mind to take action, use all of your senses.

LOVE YOUR MONEY!

TAKE OUT SOME OF YOUR MONEY (A TWENTY DOLLAR BILL OR GREATER).

LOOK AT IT - NOTICE THE DIFFERENT COLORS, THE PICTURES ON THE BILL, THE NUMBERS OR ANYTHING ELSE TO IMPRESS YOUR CREATIVE MIND THROUGH YOUR SENSE OF SIGHT.

NOW, SMELL THE MONEY - IT TRULY HAS A DISTINCTIVE FRAGRANCE. SMELL IT AGAIN TO IMPRESS YOUR CREATIVE MIND THROUGH YOUR SENSE OF SMELL.

NOW, FEEL THE MONEY - USE YOUR SENSE OF TOUCH TO FEEL THE TEXTURE, THE SMOOTHNESS OR ROUGHNESS.

NOW, HOLD THE MONEY UP TO YOUR EAR - HEAR THE CRACKLE OF THE MONEY AND THE SOUND IT MAKES AS YOU MOVE IT THROUGH YOUR FINGERS.

TAKE YOUR MONEY OUT EVERY DAY AND USE YOUR SENSES TO IMPRESS YOUR CREATIVE MIND. MAKE THE TECHNIQUE JOYFUL AND FUN, AND WITH A GRATEFUL HEART BLESS ALL YOUR MONEY AND EVERYTHING ELSE THAT IS WONDERFUL IN YOUR LIFE.

No Words Spoken Here . . .

This is another fun activity to increase your intuitive powers and to show that you do have intuition. You will have to find a friend, or if you are in a study group, this exercise is a great way to learn about one another.

Pair off and sit facing each other. Take about five minutes each to complete this exercise.

One person is the receiver and the other person is the giver. The giver places the downward turned palm of their hand on top of their partner's palm that is turned upward.

When you begin this exercise, the person receiving the energy and information states in their *mind*: I AM receptive and I AM one with Universal Consciousness. Feel yourself receiving energy and information from your partner.

The person giving the energy and information states in their *mind*: I AM giving and I AM one with Universal Consciousness. Feel yourself giving energy and information to your partner.

The receiver will begin to intuit information about their partner.

Trade roles and start the exercise again.

Discuss what you found out about each other. It is quite surprising how much we know or learn about each other without words. Ralph Waldo Emerson once said, "Who you are shouts so loudly, I can't hear you". Our energy is constantly interpreted by those around us, proving that no words need to be spoken to show who we are.

YOU WALK THROUGH WHATEVER YOU THINK!

You walk through whatever you think, so why not consciously project your thoughts to create an effortless path for yourself?

In this next exercise, you will do just that! Whatever you want accomplished, think about it *silently* in your mind.

There may be a short time lapse before an event will take place however, be patient because this exercise will convince you that your thoughts are *alive*!

Try *thinking* something as simple as, you want the perfect parking place, you want your drink refilled by your server, or you would like your friend to offer you ice cream. Just think about what you want *silently* in your mind and watch how the "universe will roll in ecstasy at your feet".

If you work with this technique consciously for a week, you will *know* without a doubt that you indeed walk through whatever you think. Then you will want to integrate this secret into your life forever, because it creates such a fun and spontaneous way to live!

6

Repetition!
Repetition!
Repetition!

"But he that of repetition is most master."
–Wallace Stevens

Words have an extraordinary impact on our creative mind, and we can change our reality through the repetition of words. Words also have tremendous power. Most people are totally unaware of this fact, so they use words to their detriment. When words are repeated over and over again this causes the creative mind to finally accept them. We learned to read and write by repeating over and over again the words our teachers gave us; we used repetition until we finally learned our ABC's. This may seem rather simple, but try it for a couple of days and you will start feeling the effects. Just remember to base your judgment on the outcome, not on some intellectual criteria.

"In the beginning was the Word."
–St. John 1:1

Repetition is the fundamental rhythm of all advancement, the heartbeat of the universe. It is the repeated self-suggestion that makes your creative mind respond, and begin to overcome any obstacles to attract what you desire. Even though the creative mind is your slave, you consciously have to play tricks on it, because it is also tremendously powerful. If an idea or word is repeated over and over again with charged emotion, then the creative mind will be influenced. Strong emotions powerfully affect the creative mind; it is the repeated self-suggestion that makes you and others believe. Anyone can demonstrate the effectiveness of the repeated word or thought, whether it is used constructively or destructively. The value of repetition has proven to be so beneficial that all you have to do is to turn on your television, read a magazine or newspaper, and see each page filled with advertising. The advertising is repeated over and over, proving that the repeated suggestion creates strong beliefs. No matter what your desire is, do this for yourself and you'll understand how repetition creates believing. The more you imagine what you want and repeat it to yourself; it will become so familiar to you, even to the point that what you want no longer seems out of reach. When we repeat the same thoughts over and over again, its creates a permanent effect. If you like the way your life is going, then you rarely examine your thoughts, but if you find yourself overcome by challenges, you begin to question what is happening to you. You can then use the power of repetition to your advantage, by repeating over and over those things you desire.

Many people are influenced by the negative words of others, and begin to believe they apply to them. The continued repetition of negative words can discourage even the most powerful and focused individual, if continued long enough. Unless you remain focused, consciously closed to negative suggestion and continue to counteract this type of thinking, you will sooner or later fall under the influence of negativity, because negativity begets negativity. We are all influenced by suggestion and repetition almost to the point of being hypnotized, because we don't consciously use our minds. We follow the same path of others who have gone before us, because everyone else is doing it. In fact, we have been following others' footsteps for decades. We hold to certain types of traditions, types of clothing, types of homes, because we are led to believe through the never ending suggestion of words that come to us from our parents, peers, news, advertisers, etc., that this is the thing to do! A mass social conditioning is seen around us in every activity. The basic secret of all successful advertising, is the continued and repeated suggestion that first makes you believe, which in turn makes you want to run out and buy!

The great doers of our world, and those who create dynamic lives are people of tremendous energy, strong imaginations, and who hold strong beliefs, so that they are not easily swayed by the collective thinking of the masses. They also take action by doing what it takes to create wealth, and making the contacts which are directed by their creative mind. Fortunes are created out of a wealth consciousness, which includes the use of the imagination, followed by action. If you consistently hold the thought that you are wealthy, then it will become true for you.

There are latent powers in the creative mind, and when understood, the world will know no boundaries, for within the creative mind lies the making of genius itself. What may seem as a mere coincidence to us, is in reality a thought that has impressed the creative mind, then transformed into physical reality. A pattern is formed in the creative mind where everything is connected, and where materialization begins by the constant repetition of your fulfilled desire. Assume the desire fulfilled, night after night!

The power of suggestion – autosuggestion (your own suggestion) or heterosuggestion (from outside sources) causes the creative mind to begin its creative work; this is where affirmations and repetition play their part. It is the repetition of the same thought and affirmation that leads to belief, and once belief becomes a deep conviction, things begin to happen. In many religions the use of the repeated word played a very important part, whether it was through prayer or mystical chants – the *force* of the repetition of words was known. The subtle force of the repeated word or suggestion overcomes reason. It begins acting directly on our feelings, and finally penetrating to the very depths of our creative mind. Through repetition, the creative mind is sensitized to the point that it works accurately to externalize the suggestion, which was most greatly impressed upon it. With this we can understand the need for constant repetition of a focused thought or idea. We can advance beyond the habitual patterns of our thinking, and also go beyond the conditioned self-images that we have of ourselves.

Listed at the end of this chapter are two techniques that will expand your awareness. The first technique is, "Enrich Your Essence & Energy". Repeat the words silently in your mind while focusing on the essence of each word. The next technique is, "Enhance Your Awareness" and the phrases are to be repeated out loud with feeling. Repetition is very important, the more consistent and faithful you are to the techniques, the stronger your creative mind becomes, and the faster your dreams materialize. At first your mind may wander because it is not used to having you in control, however continue with the techniques as it will become easier. Even if you become bored, continue repeating the words and phrases. Find a quiet place where you will not be disturbed for about twelve minutes, and meditate on the words you resonate with. Consciously use these techniques each day until the words become a part of you.

Your desires will seem more realistic to you, the more you use the law of repetition. Repetition makes your desires feel more familiar to you, thereby making it easier and easier to materialize what you want. Remember you used repetition with the limited image you had of yourself, now use your imagination and repetition for the expanded image of yourself.

If you want to start your own business or you want a better job or promotion, keep repeating to yourself constantly that you already have the perfect work. You have already visualized the perfect goal, but by means of continued repetition, you carry your desires deeply and firmly into your creative mind. Never forget the creative mind will accept and begin working on whatever you instruct it to do! Continue to think in terms of what you want, and consciously fill your mind with powerful and creative thoughts.

ENRICH YOUR
ESSENCE & ENERGY!

This list of very powerful words is to be repeated silently in your mind, preferably after you have meditated and connected with your source of power. Set aside twelve minutes each day, choose at least twelve words from the list (or twelve of your own) and slowly repeat each word silently four times in your mind. Focus on each word, feeling its energy and how it resonates with you. The words will begin to impress your creative mind and you will soon feel their effects. These words will begin to create their own path of energy, thereby changing the essence of your thoughts. You'll soon be fulfilling your desires more quickly, and releasing the many thoughts that no longer serve you.

Abundance	Achievement	Acceptance
Attention	Authentic	Awareness
Balance	Beauty	Bliss
Coherence	Compassion	Confidence
Creativity	Desire	Dynamic
Ecstasy	Elegant	Empowerment
Enchantment	Enlightenment	Enriching
Freedom	Greatness	Gratefulness

Happiness	Harmony	Honesty
Knowing	Immortality	Intelligence
Integrity	Intention	Intuition
Laughter	Love	Mastery
Opulent	Originality	Passion
Peace	Power	Prosperity
Purpose	Serenity	Sharing
Sincerity	Spirit	Strength
Success	Synchronicity	Transformation
Trust	Truth	Unboundedness
Unity	Wealth	Wisdom

Enhance Your Awareness. . .

I AM one with all good things
I AM grateful for all of my successes
I AM a strong person
I AM one with harmony
I AM one with abundance and wealth
I AM creative
I AM confident and empowered
I AM at peace
I AM the center of my power
I AM a success and everything I do is a success
I AM unlimited in my own abilities
I AM living in the present moment
I AM guided toward enriching experiences
I AM at one with joy and happiness
I AM not limited by my past thinking
I AM willing to grow
I AM at one with health, happiness and prosperity
I AM deeply loved
I AM open and receptive to new ideas of wealth
I AM open to receiving my good from unexpected sources
I AM one with tremendous wealth
I AM one with all of my needs and desires being met
I AM the only thinker in my mind
I AM free to be who I want to be

7

Follow
Your
Heart's
Desire!

"Every human mind is a great slumbering power
until awakened by a keen desire
and by definite resolution to do."
–Edgar Roberts

The essence of desire is to express life, and to express more of it! You will manifest what you want more quickly, the more passionate your desire. Desire is the motivating action behind your thought, and without an all consuming desire, nothing can be achieved or accomplished. Desire is the primary directive force in all of us; creation came about because of desire – it is the force of life! Desire is for self-expression, and life is more completely expressed through the individual who lives greatly and passionately. Your life can be magically transformed by following through on your desires.

"By annihilating the desires, you annihilate the mind.
Every man without passions has within him
no principle of action, nor motive to act."
–Claude Helvetius

Each person has their own idea of what success means to them; it may be fame, riches, knowledge, or a great position. What you want for yourself, and not what others want for you, is all that really counts, so make your objective the burning desire of your life. It is the directed thought, the belief and imagination with deep-rooted desire that convinces the creative mind of what you want.

At times you may have a certain feeling to act on something that may not even seem logical, but follow through with it. We are influenced by our desires, and by putting the great power of desire into effect, we are directing our creative mind; it begins to magnetize and orchestrate energy to make things happen.

"Desire is the essence of man."
  –Benedict Spinoza

Many schools of thought have emphasized the suppression of desire, and have attempted to convince us that the enjoyment of material things is not spiritual. In fact, to be spiritual is to renounce all that is material. It is further emphasized that if we don't do this, there is something greatly wrong with us. These theories do not understand the true nature of our spirituality, or of the greater aspects of physics. This ideology is very antiquated, so we need to change this way of thinking, and replace it with a belief system that serves us.

We are meant to experience all the abundance of life and to enjoy the fruits of our efforts. The concept of refuting the physical dimension to achieve nirvana or heaven, is to deny who we are. If we are constantly denying our desires, then why are we here? Aren't the teachings that promote this way of thinking not in fact, *desiring* to be "desire-less"?

These philosophies also emphasize the importance of the different levels of consciousness, while shunning the conscious mind. We have a conscious mind, so that we can be individual and choose. Diversity is what consciousness is all about. It is not natural to live with these concepts, because they promote an artificial means of living with guilt. This type of guilt is distorted to justify a type of mood making, while denying the essence of our own being and the strong yearnings of our soul to experience life! Denying our very natural desires to experience life to the fullest, is to cheat us out of our inherent right to express who we are. There is no separation between the mind and the body; they are both born of spirituality. We have said that the mind is the subjective experience of consciousness and the body is the objective experience. We need to encourage the concept of reaching toward full human potential, which in turn will contribute to the betterment and creativity of the human race. Desire is the soul's way of learning, experiencing, growing, evolving, and enjoying goes along with that too!

Everything we have in our world today is the result of desire. Desire brings about change, for example; poverty creates the desire for riches, hunger creates the desire for food, and weakness creates the desire for power. Thomas Edison tried twenty thousand different materials before finding one that he could use for the light bulb. It was *desire* that spurred Mr. Edison to continue with his inventions, and if he hadn't listened to his inner desires, we wouldn't be enjoying the benefits of his inventions today! And where would we be today, if Mr. John Crapper hadn't acted upon his desires?

Therefore act on your desires, because acting on your desires is the cause behind everything you experience and accomplish.

> "You are what your deep driving desire is,
> As your desire is, so is your will,
> As your will is, so is your deed,
> As your deed is, so is your destiny.
> –Brihadaranyaka Upanishad IV.

Therefore, begin with desire, add the magic of believing, and you can create your own script. Make it a quality script; you are the author, the producer, the director, and the actor. The author has the desire, the producer coordinates the desire, the director oversees the desire, and the actor rehearses the desire over and over again, until his part is natural, and the desire is fulfilled.

Let's Work On That Creative Mind!

This exercise allows you to gain a deeper understanding of how your imagination works. You will gain a deeper understanding of how you see yourself now and how you can make changes.

Fold the paper in half and on the left side of the page title **"How I Was"** write down how your present life situation is. On the right side of the paper titled **"How I Am Now"** write down how you want to see yourself in the future (even though it is stated it as now).

How I Was   **How I Am Now**

8

May
I
Have
Your
Attention,
Please!

> "One of the strongest characteristics of genius
> is the power of lighting its own fire."
> –John Foster

Attention is very important, as it directs the energy of what you want. Whatever you desire, put your attention on it, and your creative mind will activate the energy to manifest it. Attention has great organizing power, so continually keep what you want lively in your awareness and your creative mind will create synchronicity in your life. Since matter and energy are interchangeable, doesn't it make sense to focus your attention on what you want, so that the energy translates into matter?

I wanted to attend a course that would cost me $1,800.00, but I had already spent an enormous amount of money on previous courses, so I decided that I would go if I could create the money. I had a desire to attend an estate sale (even though I seldom ever went to one), so I purchased a weekend newspaper. I noticed a huge ad as I was looking through the classified section that indicated an estate sale would be starting at 8:00 in the morning the next day. It stated that this was to be the estate sale of the decade! There certainly were magnificent items for sale, as the lady who was liquidating all of her possessions had impeccable taste. I talked my husband into going with me, and when we arrived many items had already been sold. I did however, notice a beautiful baby grand piano that had a sale sticker on it for $2,600.00. I looked over the piano and it was in excellent condition. I asked my husband what he thought of the piano, and he agreed that the piano was at least worth the $2,600.00, if not more. We decided to submit a bid for $1,800.00 however before doing this, we first used our imaginations, and envisioned our bid being accepted. Our bid was accepted on the condition that we would have the piano moved within two days. I began calling movers and found one that had the time available to move the piano that day for $250.00. I gave the movers the address, but I didn't think to tell them that there were twenty very steep stairs to the home where the piano was located. The piano movers took one look at the stairs, turned around, got into their truck, and without saying a word, drove off. Even though I was a bit bewildered, I again started calling other piano movers and found a mover that could move the piano the next day. I told them about the steep stairs, and they felt there would be no problem. Instead of their normal fee of $100.00, there would be an additional charge of $25.00 for the inconvenience of the stairs. I thought this truly is magical, not only did I find a wonderful moving company, but I was also charged $125.00 less then I was quoted from the other company. After I had the piano moved to my home, I began investigating the worth of my new acquisition. I found it had sold for $7,500.00 when it was new, and was now worth $4,000.00. Bingo! I placed an ad in the classified section of our local newspaper, and sold the piano the following weekend for $3,700.00. This gave me the money I needed to attend the seminar. This proved to me that by focusing my attention on what I wanted, not only brought about quite interesting details; it also proved I could achieve greater results. Continue to be aware of opportunities, because many times our limited thinking leads us to believe that the only place we can receive money, is through our present occupation, and this simply is not so. There have been many incidents where I have made or received money from places that were not in any way related to my career.

Attention creates coherency, and a more coherent thought is very powerful. When our thoughts are coherent, they are as if in tune with each other, rather then canceling each other out, they work together to produce what you want. Put your attention on your emotionally charged thoughts, and you will marvel how easily your desires are accomplished. Practice the wonderful discipline of putting your attention on harmonious and constructive thoughts; focus on wealth, prosperity, money, health, and wonderful relationships. You can better understand by the events that took place in my life, how the creative mind goes about organizing what you want, just by putting your attention on your desires.

9

Believe
It
Or
Not!

"Believe that you have and you have it."
–Old Proverb

A belief is a personal thought that an individual has conclusively drawn about themselves, or others. It becomes the framework that an individual will use, to perceive their environment, their relationships with others, and about life in general. In other words, what we have come to believe about ourselves and others, directs us to certain actions, and because we believe so thoroughly about certain concepts, others will tend to believe that about us as well.

Beliefs are like a hypnotic force. Your constant inner thinking reinforces your beliefs, and in turn your creative mind readily accepts those beliefs as your only reality. Therefore, what you believe has been thought by you repeatedly, but if you have been like most individuals, you have not even thought about or questioned the how, or why of your belief patterns. A belief is usually sustained in your consciousness until something happens to make you question it. With this understanding, you then know that you can consciously make the changes you desire by simply changing your thoughts and beliefs about yourself.

To bring about a shift in your experiences all you have to do is to concentrate your energy in the present moment, and consciously introduce new beliefs to replace your old ones. Remember, you come directly face to face with the full impact of your beliefs, so begin by suspending certain beliefs. Focus on your desired goal to create a new belief pattern. Take a few minutes each day, to use the natural technique of self-suggestion to focus your attention on your newly designed belief. Feeling the new belief, visualizing the new belief, and repeating it over and over again, will accelerate the acceptance of the new belief. Beliefs direct your experience, and self-suggestion is just a means of focused attention, which helps to lock out unwanted distractions.

Based upon your current beliefs, you will attract certain experiences into your life. You will draw others to you, or seek out certain experiences according to your specialized beliefs. You form your future *now* through your beliefs, so keep in mind the very powerful knowledge that your point of *power* is in the *present*. There is absolutely no reason for you to continue to project into your future, the undesirable events that have happened to you in the past. Your experiences are being created moment by moment, and your present beliefs create your future events. You have selected your experiences that form your reality, and a realization of this allows you to make the necessary changes that seem impossible. You will begin to achieve those greater and more fulfilling experiences you do want. Your experiences will change automatically when your beliefs change. When you change your beliefs, you activate new energy and power to create your new experiences. You attune to different frequencies while locking out the old ones. This magnetizes new events, which in time will become your newly created reality. Depending on how strong your desires and beliefs are, will be the determining factor of how fast they will materialize. Begin by expanding your beliefs, so that you tap into the infinite treasure-house of opportunities, and you will experience wealth beyond your present reality.

Again, refrain from using your past as a point of reference, instead restructure events by using your imagination to create successful events. Many times an individual will look to the past, and only focus on their disappointments. This is actually a distorted picture of the past, because it doesn't contain the good or happy experiences that existed. You always sustain those events that you continually focus upon, and your experiences will continue to mirror how you feel about past events. Many of us have been taught to focus only on the negative aspect of our lives, because our role models were afraid to desire great things for themselves, simply because they were afraid of disappointment. Many individuals think it makes no sense to change, because they can't overcome their negative thinking anyway. They are fully convinced that negative thoughts are more powerful, but remember it is their *belief* that negative thoughts are more powerful. When you begin to create a new belief pattern look to your past with new eyes, and create new perceptions, so that you can change that which seems to justify your old beliefs. You must consciously make some type of effort, be willing to make the changes you need, and to stop being at the mercy of your past beliefs! What you continually believe closes the door to other probabilities or opportunities that would naturally be open to you. Those other opportunities are literally invisible to you! When you open up your mind, you also open the door to extraordinary experiences.

We have to trust that what we want will come about, and for this to happen we also have to believe with every fiber of our being, and crave it passionately. Belief intensifies your desire, and leads the creative mind to bring into reality what you believe to be true. Keep what you want active in your consciousness, and this will set the law of attraction into motion, to bring about the changes you want. The changes will take place, even though there appears to be no known explanation. Even if you have feelings of doubt and fear, just state what you want, and trust that it will happen. Having trust, means to be definite in your thought, and keeping a steady attitude that your desires are already fulfilled. You do not hope something will happen, because hope keeps your desires in the future.

Thinking is not passive; it is active! Change your focus of awareness and see what happens. It is difficult for the average person to concentrate for any length of time. You will find that thoughts, ideas and desires, come and go quickly; you are always giving your creative mind confused messages, and if you are not consciously aware, you will be continually influenced by outside sources. You will experience synchronicity when you give your creative mind a clear and dynamic image of your desire. However, you must first believe that you can have what you want; if you think you have to convince others, you are not convinced yourself, as much as you believe with all your heart, the law is set into motion. Before you take any type of action, affirm in your mind that you have what you want. If you want a specific event to take place, sit quietly and think that it is complete. This way your experiences will come to you effortlessly, because your thoughts allow the event to open. Try this before you start out your day, and the events will emerge as if by magic!

What beliefs do you hold about yourself concerning wealth or poverty? Many individuals believe that riches are given, or taken away by an angry or benevolent god, or by some external force that has control over their lives. This simply is not true! They often feel hardships are thrust upon them as one of life's lessons.

Many beliefs are carried to extreme, even to the point that many feel their good fortune rides on some external ritual or old myth. You may think that carrying a rabbit's foot, clicking your heels twice, crossing your fingers or whatever ritual, will bring you good luck. All rituals that seemingly bring good luck are nothing other then your *focused belief* that an object, or certain behavior will bring about a specific action in your life.

Individuals throughout history have created great myths to explain their experiences. Myths are perceptions surrounding certain types of behavior that have been created to bridge the unknown, which has not been understood. It's your *imagination* that leads you to the belief that you are poor, because of something evil that has happened to you. Consciousness is much greater, and we can indeed create a more expansive belief system; one where we don't blame some external force, or believe that every event we encounter is some lesson we are destined to experience, because the planet Earth is a school. We create our own reality and this is the only lesson!

Your beliefs direct your actions; you feel happy, upset or elated based upon your *beliefs* about certain situations. You will not understand why you feel the way you do, until you understand what you believe. It may seem that you are feeling happy or upset about some event, because of external influences, rather it is your belief about the event that creates those feelings. Your inner beliefs need to be determined, and this will show you who you are, and why you are experiencing certain events.

"The life which is unexamined is not worth living."
–Socrates

Again, you direct your creative mind with your beliefs, which is the producer of all your experiences. The greatest secret to enlightenment, is the realization that through your conscious thoughts and beliefs, you create your own reality. Your physical life is created by your choices, and you can consciously create a life that is filled with exceptional experiences as you play an infinity of roles.

The more conscious you become concerning your thoughts, the more capable you become to create what you want. You must accept the responsibility that you create your own reality, and that your challenges are the result of your own state of consciousness.

Only the aware mind can change it's beliefs, and enlightenment is the result of an expanded consciousness. Learn to consciously create, and break out of the self-limiting behavior that keeps your energy blocked, your thoughts and beliefs stagnated. Within you lies all the wisdom that you will ever need, to create a life of abundance and enrichment. This incredible power within you can overcome any challenge, so honor it and use it.

10

Play
It
Again,
Sam!

"The past is never dead,
not even is it past."
–King Ramses II

The past is not finished; it is open ended, and can be changed by changing your present beliefs. Science has proven that all transformations of power are reversible; energy and matter, action and reaction, cause and effect, because at the quantum level they are all the same. In fact, heat produces energy, and energy produces heat; electricity produces magnetism, and magnetism produces electricity. This shows that the power of reversibility exists, therefore it is possible to apply the same principles to revise our past.

Let's take the following example; if you received a letter in the mail and you didn't like what it said, rewrite it *mentally*, imagining that this was the letter you received. Continue doing this until you have revised the past event. You create your own reality, and you are one with whatever you think about most. The truth is that you can exert your ideals over anything physical, as long as it is in keeping with integrity, and the laws of nature. By now, you know that your reality is created by your thought, and the thought that you entertain in the present moment, is the only one that counts. All physical or space time events take place in the present moment; this is how you can alter a theme already in existence, when it pertains to you. Any other thought that isn't in existence, is only the memory of the past, or an imagined event of the future. You can indeed transcend what most think of as the law of cause and effect. Each event you experience, is held in its own space and time. This shows us that time is not really linear or successive, which makes change possible; you are not held to what you think of as a definite outcome from a past action. Time and space are merely constructs of thought; you can transform thought through your imagination to change certain events. Everything exists first in consciousness, and physical reality, is nothing other then the out-picturing of your thoughts.

Your physical self according to your senses, is the only solid part of consciousness. This is the only part of you that dwells in space and time. Your consciousness however, is free to go back and forth in time. We are not yet knowledgeable enough yet to accept this, so we think that whatever has happened cannot be revised. But we really are not limited, and when we begin to expand our awareness, we open new doors of opportunity. A new belief in the present causes a change in your past at the quantum level. The quantum level consists only of energy and information. When we focus our attention on an event past or present, we can indeed make the revisions we want. Until we focus our attention, certain events remain unchanged or continue to just be probabilities. It is also very important not to obsess about a past event; change it, and any negative circumstances by introducing new energy and information. Integrate this idea completely, so that you know without a doubt that you create your reality.

A friend of mine wanted to work for a particular company, advocating a persistently firm course of action, so I suggested that she use the secrets for wealth given in my book. Prior to applying for a position, she began to envision being called by the Vice President, and offered a position with the company. Even after she applied and interviewed several times for the job, she continued seeing herself as already working for the company. Two weeks later, she received a telephone call stating that she had *not* been selected. She called me saying that she did everything I suggested, but didn't understand what she did wrong. I told her that she had to revise the telephone call in her *imagination*, and affirm that she was hired. She continued to do so, and one week later she received a call from the Vice President. He asked her if she would be willing to come in, to meet with him and a manager from another department. She met with them and was told a new division in their R&D department had been created, but they had to wait for approval before the position could be filled. He offered her the new position, and she just about fell out of her chair, as this was better then she had thought possible.

Relive the day as you wanted it, by consciously reconstructing the events with new content, and you will revise the past. Imagine the new event, and see those involved responding to you in a new way. This part is very important, because you are sending them a new message telepathically. You are in essence sending out your thoughts, changing the terms and behavior of your relationship. Now, some individuals will respond to the message and will make the necessary changes, while others will want to remain in the old pattern. They will no longer be a part of your experience. You can only make changes concerning your life, so understand that some will gladly be a part of your life by changing, and others will go onto different experiences; a change however, will take place, and the change had to begin within you. When your belief changes, your life and those around you will change also.

By inserting into the present new ideas about your past, you can and will create changes both physically and psychologically. The past is not concrete even though it seems that way to you; it is just a conversion of energy and information. Remember your thoughts and ideas are just as alive as you are. The point of power is in the present, and when you focus your attention in the present, you alter the previous energy and information; what you wanted changed, now becomes an entirely new event. When you are focused in the moment – your point of power – a magical transformation takes place.

11

What
Do
You
Want!

"There is only one success, to be able
to spend your life in your own way."
–Christopher Morley

Now write down how much money you will make this year. Each time you do this exercise, a certain amount immediately comes to mind. This amount reveals the mental equivalent that you have regarding wealth. The amount you wrote down, is in direct correlation to what you experience in life. If you wrote down a conservative amount of money, this reveals the mental limitations that you have. The creative mind orchestrates exactly what a person thinks of themselves without question, whether they are aware of this or not. Those who can't get ahead in life are generally not aware of this great secret for wealth and success. People who are successful are indeed most aware of this, and have done their utmost to work on their self-image.

Most people are afraid to work through their mental limitations, because they are used to going without. They are convinced that wealth and success are not for them, or they don't need much anyway. They have become afraid to dream and they have made their limitations into a habit. The exercise at the end of this chapter titled, "One Hundred Sows & Bucks" will allow you to change those limiting patterns you have created for yourself. Before reading any further, complete the exercise by following the directions. After you have completed it, return to this chapter and continue reading the next paragraph.

The first amount you wrote down is how you see yourself. The amount represents to the penny how much you think you are worth, whether you are willing to admit it or not. If you put down a conservative number, you may think you are being reasonable, but in truth you don't believe you are worth much. You may think that this way of thinking is justified, but this is exactly the type of thinking that keeps you limited. What you wrote down, is a mirror image of what you think about yourself, and what you think you are entitled to. If you want change, then you have to discard your limited thinking.

How can you expand your thinking, your boundaries, and throw off your self-imposed limitations? Begin by writing down an amount, and continue increasing the amounts you write down. When you become used to seeing greater amounts in writing, your creative mind will be influenced to start making changes. Write down greater and greater amounts, make the amounts grand; if you're going to do it, do it grand! This exercise is very powerful in helping you to develop a wealth consciousness. When you become accustomed to greater amounts of money, your conscious mind will not fight against what you want. You are conditioning it to see greater opportunities for you, and it will begin to accept this more readily.

The written word has a very powerful impact on us, and if we see something in writing, we tend to accept it. By the same token if we are not used to seeing something, we tend to reject it. Words don't even have to be true to have an effect on us. By using our imagination and the power of words, we can shape our reality.

"Character equals destiny."
–Heraclitus

Successful people know they create with their thoughts, and they are undaunted by outer appearances; they continue to hold true to their vision, even though what they face may seem insurmountable.

When you learn the value of your thoughts, you will work on directing your thoughts for your greater good. The stronger your character becomes, and the more dedicated you are to your vision, the quicker you will accomplish your goals, even beyond your greatest expectations! Those who continue to firmly believe that they create their own success with their thoughts, are very dynamic individuals that others find irresistible. There are millions of talented and creative people, whose achievements could contribute so much to our evolution, because they are not aware of the power of thought, they go on struggling and live dissatisfied lives.

How do you find the blocks you have, and the limitations you have set for yourself? First, begin with the amount you wrote down, this amount directly corresponds with what you think you are worth. The great obstacle to your success has been your thinking, so expand your thinking and you will experience change.

We get exactly what we ask for, so the very first thing you need to determine is, what do you want most out of life, and be specific. Merely stating that you want to be rich is too vague. Write it down! Let your imagination go – let yourself dream! To get rich, you have to begin dreaming. Many people just don't know what they want, so how can they accomplish anything in life? They are unable to tell you how much money they want to make, what they want to do with their life, or what kind of possessions they want. The very simple act of listing your dreams and desires, begins the first step to transforming your reality. When you write down your objectives, the creative mind starts its organizing power to translate your desires into reality. If you feel a desire to act on something do so, as this may be the creative mind urging you to seize an opportunity. Before you take any kind of action, ask yourself one question, "Is this right for me?", and if you listen to your heart intelligence, you will know without a doubt whether to pursue the opportunity. A feeling or impression will come up letting you know that you are making the right decision. Be open and aware, for if you give into your fear, you block your judgment, which prevents you from realizing your dreams.

Those who have no set objective are putting their energy into everything. Many times, they are influenced by the thoughts of others which creates confusion, so they end up with nothing. Those who have set definite objectives tune into one frequency, so if they want money that is what they get, or if they want a certain career, that is what they get. Whether you set your mind on something large or small, great riches or a house in the country, you give it energy. As long as you give it your energy, you will draw it to you. The intensity of your desire, determines how fast you will materialize what you want. If you direct your energy toward many things, your energy becomes divided, and this results in a lower reaction time. So, focus your energy on one goal, a goal that may encompass many other goals, then go onto the next goal and so on. If at times doubt arises, hold fast to your desires, because you will succeed. It is only a matter of time before you will achieve wealth, and be living your dream.

You will become master of your destiny, and isn't that secretly what you want?

Be thoughtful about the questions in the exercise at the end of this chapter titled, "What Do I Want?" because what you answer will start to determine your future. The questions are really about finding out who you are, and only one out of a hundred people will take the time to find out what makes them happy, let alone even think about what they really want.

When a person in our society (which is given over so much to the pursuit of money) doesn't have money, their tendency is to feel inferior because their self-esteem is equated with earning power. Unfortunately, this belief has greatly affected the men in our culture. However, we can increase our self-worth in our minds, by believing that as a human being our worth is much greater then the sum total of our money; realize we are so much greater that it can't be measured.

When you stop identifying with a certain state of mind, and introduce something new, then your life begins to change. Our society believes that hard work is the only way a person can make it. But, doesn't hard work seem oppressive and offer no way out? What if we encouraged an individual to seek work that is fulfilling for them, where their creative needs are met – is that hard work?

When we are happy, and our self-esteem is high, then we are unlikely to exhibit behavior that is addictive or unhealthy for ourselves. In fact, many experts will insist emphatically that a person must live with a certain type of behavior for the rest of their lives, when nothing could be further from the truth. Every experience we have is not absolute, and we don't have to carry around behaviors that no longer serve us. We can just let them go, and not give them any more energy. We can change, but in order to change, we have to find out what makes us happy, and what our creative talents are. Society prefers to lump everyone into one neat category, rather then find out what qualities each person shows.

People in general are afraid of change, and therefore prefer to stay within the status quo. Many individuals remain stuck in limited perspectives, actually they are knowledgeable only in a specific field. They do not continue to learn new information that could indeed contribute to improvement for themselves, and for society. It is time we break the mold, and become more expansive in our thinking. Whatever you state I AM with that is what you will align your energies with. When the actions of your thought correspond with the actions you will physically perform, reality is created. It is not the facts that shape our lives, it is what we dream it to be!

ONE HUNDRED SOWS & BUCKS

This is an exercise to have you expand your boundaries. Begin by writing down how much you will make this year.

Now, expand your thinking and boundaries by increasing the amount you write down.

Continue doing this, making the amount greater and greater.

Remember, when your creative mind sees greater and greater amounts, you will be breaking down limitations!

MAKE iT BiG BUCKS!!!

The Check's on Me!

Here's your chance to say "The Check's on Me"! You have an unlimited amount of money in your account at the Millionare's Bank. You can feel completely free to spend your money on that special someone, or you can write the check for that very expensive luxury item you want. It's up to you! Write it for anything and any amount you want!

$$$$$

No. 1000

Date_____

Pay to the order of_____ $_____

Amount_____

Millionares Bank
One Mastery Lane
Anytown, USA $$$$$

For_____ Signature_____

What Do You Want?

1. What are your dreams and desires? List only one or two of your greater desires, because many of your other desires can be achieved by reaching your greater ones._____

_____

_____

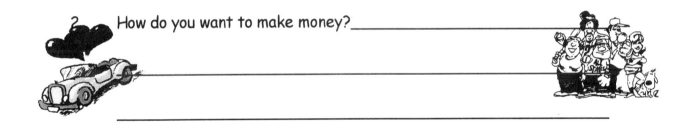

2. How do you want to make money?_____

_____

_____

3. How much money do you want?_____

_____

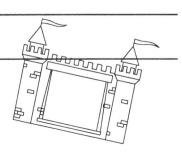

12

Sleep
On
It!

"In a dream, in a vision of the night,
when deep sleep falleth upon men,
in slumberings upon the bed, then he openeth
the ears of men, and sealeth their instruction."
–Job 33:15-16

By now, you have learned that the great power lies in consciously thinking of what you want. We also know that the creative mind continues to work even while you are asleep, or while you are relaxing. An effective way to introduce what you want to your creative mind, is to take some time for relaxation either through meditation, or a daydream. Just prior to this, think of your desires and allow them to seep into your creative mind. Many times if you had fallen asleep while seeking an answer to something, you would have received a solution upon waking.

My experience has shown me, if I continue to use my imagination, and believe that what I want is true for me, it will turn into fact. The following story illustrates this; my husband and I had been living in a condo, and I wanted to move into a home, but everything I looked at just didn't seem to be what I wanted. Night after night, I would look at the homes across the way from where we lived, and I would fall asleep on the belief that I was already living in my new home.

A friend of ours was moving back to Denver, and needed a place to live. At that time we were leasing the condo, so I asked my landlord if he had anything available to rent, and he told me about a home with a lease/purchase. The home was in the exact location I had been viewing, so I went to see it, as it turned out our friend leased the condo we were living in, and we moved into the home. This event has convinced me that we can have anything we please, if we will make it a habit, and think *from* the desired end.

Before going into a relaxed state, visualize that you are the architect drawing up the plans and life designs to make the changes you want. Fall asleep while imagining from the newly designed concept of yourself.

Tremendous shifts in consciousness take place when you are in a restful or sleeping state. In fact, the most powerful changes take place when you have retreated from physical reality. Energy and information are reorganized, and changed according to your state of mind; certain probabilities are calculated and balanced when you are in a calm state, and least aware.

In the dream state, a dimension where you can express greater flexibility, you try out thoughts and beliefs to see how they will fit into your waking reality. Dreams are full of information concerning the state of your present reality, and they can also give you many wonderful insights into your present conditions. Actually dreams provide you with a framework in which you can explore various probabilities, giving you valuable information about which events to act on. In the dream state, you transcend obstacles and limitations allowing your consciousness to act out fantasies or desires that may, or may not work in your waking reality. If you are having a difficult time finding the answer you are seeking, your consciousness will begin to search through the dream state for the one that will work. In dreams, you receive information that you may have been too distracted to receive in the waking state.

Many times we do not remember our dreams, but the information is however, assimilated and integrated by the creative mind. The creative mind will reserve this information until it is needed. Many times when you come up with "a bright idea" it was actually formed while you were dreaming.

In the dream state your conscious mind is subdued, which in the waking state may act as an obstacle to the changes you want to make. You are free to try out the new belief in a rich interplay of energies. You may be focused on one particular event, and until this is worked out in consciousness, you may have recurring dreams. You will experience clarity, or a direct solution to the events in your waking life.

Before you enter the dream state, give yourself the suggestion that you need to know you are dreaming, and you want an answer to your question. Using dreams in this fashion can provide you with an invaluable tool to work with.

If you want to change your relationship with someone, just state what you want changed, and give yourself the suggestion that this will be accomplished in the dream state. In your dreams you can contact those who are not willing to make the changes in waking life, or those you are unable to talk to. This technique allows you to express yourself freely with those you want to make changes with. Always request an answer to anything you want resolved in your life.

Only you have the ability to interpret your dreams correctly. There is no universal meaning for a dream symbol, even though many individuals believe there are, because dreams are just as individual as you are. Dreams are based upon your waking experiences, and no two individuals will ever have the same experience. You can however, learn to interpret your own dream symbols, and this will unlock the door to a very powerful way that will awaken your intuition, your knowing, and also give you the insight you need to act on.

Your dreams can give you valuable knowledge, and when you truly believe this, you will gain considerable freedom. Let's say you have a decision to make, but you are on the fence about it. Just before you take some time to slip into a drowsy state, introduce your question. You will receive an answer, which may come to you simply as a sense of knowing, or a desire to take action.

In the dream state we are not confined to space or time, and it is here that we can access the field of infinite probabilities. In this less restricted dimension, we may go from one drama to the next, working out all the possible variations to the events we want changed. Your dreams may not seem clear to you, because you are not used to consciously examining your beliefs. When you understand what your beliefs are, you will be able to use the dream state more effectively. Even nightmares allow you to work out many unacknowledged beliefs, or unexpressed energies, in turn giving you the best solution to an event that has been a mystery to you.

Your mind is not only affected by your dreams, but your body is too! Many times healings can take place; what is commonly termed as a spontaneous remission can occur, or a solution to an imbalance in the body will come forth.

The ancients created dream catchers because they knew the value of dreams. They knew dreams provided great insights into many areas of their lives, thereby creating dramatic changes and enhancing creative solutions. They also knew that they created their own reality, and that reality could be altered through the nature of dreams.

SWEET DREAMS!

Imagine what you want in your life, and do this either before you are about to go to sleep for the night, or when you have time to take a short nap. The length of sleep is not important, but going to sleep while thinking *from* your desired state, solidifies it.

Sit quietly, becoming very relaxed even a little drowsy, and imagine that you are already living your fulfilled dream. Enter your desired state as though you are the actor, not just standing back and merely looking on; *feeling* that you are actually performing the imagined event, so that it becomes real to you. Choose one desire that you want to make as your reality such as receiving money, sitting in a room in your new home or driving your new car. Continue imagining your perfect state and feel it's reality as you fall asleep, you will truly be amazed at how events will take place.

If you are one that has difficulty in visualizing events, then just say in your mind that you are happy and thankful for whatever it is you desire. Use the technique that best suits you in bringing about the changes you want. Be sure after you have used this technique that you do not cancel out your good by wondering if, or when events will take place.

In our *imagination* we have to live the life we want, and abandon the state we are in. *This is a great secret!* We have to love our new state of existence that we have imagined, and give no more attention to the present state we are in. Do not become interlocked in your environment.

WHAT A DAY FOR A DAYDREAM. . .

Imagine that you are granted one wish that will magically change some aspect of your life.

Think about something in your life that you have thought about changing, either past or present. Take some time to daydream about what you want!

Now, illustrate or describe the new change that has taken place.

This activity really enlivens your imagination and activates the power of attraction to bring about your desires.

Remember if you think you are not creative, the only difference between you and a highly creative person, is the constant use of the imagination!

127

AND THE ANSWER iS . . .

WRITE DOWN ANY CHALLENGES YOU ARE EXPERIENCING AND JUST BEFORE FALLING ASLEEP ASK FOR AN ANSWER. KEEP THIS SHEET ON YOUR NIGHTSTAND, SO THAT UPON WAKING YOU CAN RECORD ANY IDEAS OR INSIGHTS THAT YOU RECEIVE.

CHALLENGE_____

_____

_____

_____

ANSWER_____

_____

_____

_____

13

Can
You
Keep
A
Secret?

"The human heart has hidden treasure,
In secret kept, in silence sealed."
–Charlotte Bronte

There is great value in keeping your dreams a secret, and this cannot be too strongly emphasized for several reasons. Keeping a secret holds your thought for you, and allows you to maintain the necessary momentum needed, to manifest your desire. When you discuss your desires with others, you release the energy the creative mind needs to build on, in order to crystallize what you want. It is very important to value secretiveness surrounding your desires, because others may say something to counteract your thoughts. If others were to entertain negativity or envy surrounding your success, this cannot only weaken your resolve, but if you are not consciously holding fast to your dreams, it can neutralize them as well. It also takes courage to tell another that your desires are fulfilled before they become a reality, so it is best to be secretive about your desires to protect the energy you are building up.

"Three may keep a secret if two of them are dead."
–Benjamin Franklin

Let's use the radio as a metaphor; the radio is an instrument that you use to tune into a certain frequency (radio station), and when it is tuned in properly it receives clear signals and what you hear is clear. When the radio is not tuned in properly, the signals are weak and you receive static. You may have even said to someone, when you tried to get something accomplished, "They just gave me static"! Well, if others tell you that what you want is impossible, they are giving you static, and you would have to use great energy to counteract their thoughts, to keep tuned in. Why not just keep your desires and dreams to yourself, so that your creative mind knows clearly what you want. It begins to start work immediately on your desires, but if you are unsure about your dreams and continually change your mind, it goes back and forth trying to create what you want; it keeps you in a static position. You will never get anywhere, because your dreams and desires have to be firmly tuned into. Keeping a secret helps you to keep focused, so that you are not unduly influenced by others, and also keeps the unnecessary doubt out of your creative mind.

"To keep a secret is wisdom."
–Samuel Johnson

The only exception to keeping a secret, would be if the person you wish to share your ideas and dreams with, feels the same way you do. Work together on what you both want, but then focus *silently* within, keeping your thoughts, desires and dreams locked inside, so that the energy builds until materialization is complete. The energy is actually accelerated by two of you directing your thoughts toward the same goal, but you each must have the *last* thought in your mind.

14

Love
What
You
Do!

"Love is a canvas furnished by Nature
and embroidered by imagination."
–Voltaire

You will achieve, and probably even surpass your most cherished desires with the secrets you are learning. However, during your journey toward wealth remember to maintain an innocent and happy attitude. If you become obsessed with the pursuit of wealth, your obsession can prevent you from enjoying life, and happiness. You do not want your success to become your identity. The reason we want wealth in the first place, is because we think by having and enjoying the many pleasures it can bring to us, we in turn will be happy. When people start earning big money, they become afraid of losing it. If you understand the power of your creative mind, you'll never have to be fearful of losing money, fame or possessions, because you'll always be able to create anything you want in your life.

In order to be happy, you have to work at something you love. People who don't like what they do, are not happy. They spend time wishing they were somewhere else, or wishing for a better life. Instead of just wishing, begin now by repeating to yourself that you can change, that change is created within, and the point of power is in the present moment. You can make major changes in your life through the simple act of changing your thinking. If you think you cannot possibly make changes, remember not to limit your view of life by your past experiences. The possibility of change, is inherent within the ability to imagine something better for yourself, so focus on your desire until it becomes a tangible reality.

"Oh, she is just in it for the money"! How many times have you heard that statement? This is usually a projection on the part of the person making the statement, because isn't that what the majority of society is doing? Working at jobs they dislike, because they need or want to make money? How many parents and role models have coached their children to choose a profession just for the money? Don't be too quick to accuse another of doing something for money before you take an inventory of your life. Are you working at a job or several jobs for that matter, just for the money? In fact, according to a survey that asked people if they would stay on their job if they weren't being paid, 80% said they would quit!

So, what is the solution? Begin by thinking of what you love to do, and how you can offer those talents in exchange for money. What changes will you need to make in your life? Focus your attention on what you want, allowing your thoughts to gather power and expand, and you will be directed in ways to accomplish your dream.

"Whatever you can do, or dream you can, begin it.
Boldness has genius, power, and magic in it.
Begin it now."
–Goethe

Would you change your plans for today, if you knew you only had twenty four hours to live? Would you do something entirely different with your life, rather then what you've been doing up until now? Ask your family and friends this question, and they will answer you in one of two ways. The ones who enjoy their lives wouldn't change a thing, because their work is their passion, and the others would be doing something entirely the opposite. Why would anyone continue living a life they don't like? True intelligence is recognizing what your talents and passions are, and to begin consciously creating a space for yourself to use those talents. Really think about the following statement, "Am I doing what I love, or am I being untrue to myself by doing something I really don't like"? If you are like most people you will just go along in life, and think that you'll make the change tomorrow, but before you know it, old age has set in; you have to this point, lived a most uneventful life. Therefore, the secret to happiness, is to live each day as if it were your last; to live each day with passion and purpose, by doing what you love to do! Passion and purpose equal life!

Right now make a commitment to yourself that you refuse to continue living, without having taken the courage to live the way you want to. Don't let your fears keep you from discovering your true passion, and living your dream. Dare to live! Too many individuals have once had great dreams, but because they didn't take action, their dreams are now just shadows of yesterday's thoughts.

Ask yourself the following question, "If I had all the money in the world, would I continue doing what I am doing now"? If the answer is no, then you need to discover what your hidden talents are and what you would like to do, because you don't like what you are doing right now. If you answered yes, then you have found your passion, and you are either experiencing great wealth and happiness, or you are on your way! To be happy and wealthy, you must enjoy what you do for your work.

Those who work at a job they dislike are jeopardized twofold, because not only do they dislike their work, but even worse, they aren't getting wealthy doing it. Why? Because they are unaware of the secrets for wealth, and they don't believe they can become a success. Their fears betray them, and keep them from ever truly becoming rich, by clinging to a type of material security that is mediocre at best. They believe that they don't have what it takes to be wealthy, or they believe that true abundance is reserved for the elite few. They have been tricked by repeated suggestions from role models, society, peers, or even their own internal chatter, which has conditioned their mind to believe the illusion that wealth is not for them. Remember, you cannot commit yourself to work that you do not love. Also, keep in mind that whatever activity you engage in, you give a part of your life energy to, so if you are working at a job that you dislike, it will deplete your energy. When you work at something you love, it will give energy back to you; you will even find you become so involved in what you are doing that you lose all track of time, and even become oblivious to your surroundings. Until you begin working at what your heart desires, the secret is to act and live your dream in your *imagination,* until it becomes true. You can predetermine your future by your imaginal activity, *feeling* in your heart the dream come true.

Many times we have difficulty recognizing our talents, gifts and qualities. Now, ask yourself the following questions. How am I distinctive? How I am special and different? What qualities can I bring to any relationship I encounter?

We all have value, so we need to start looking at ourselves to gain clarity, and awareness of our creative talents. If we don't know what they are, how can we show others, or even have others value us? Unless we acknowledge our value, no one will see the value either.

You have extraordinary and innate qualities that are uniquely your own, and it is up to you to acknowledge this then silently project it to others. There is an old saying that others will know who you are because you project who you are. Others will begin to sense something unique about you and be automatically attracted to you without knowing why; you will be the type of individual that people notice. At your work, between your family and friends, and even strangers will sense an exceptional quality about you. You will become an enigma to others, a sheer mystery when you understand your value and master these secrets.

There are several things you can do to build your confidence, and understand the value you have to offer. Ask your family or friends what they believe are your best qualities and strengths. Ask them to be honest about what they see in you. Keep asking until you get a sense of your value, a value you may not have thought amounted to much. This may even be uncomfortable for you because society has taught us to ignore our creativity, and you may feel that you don't have any talents.

You really need to find, and instill the value within yourself then honor that value when you are providing a service for someone. Set down how much you want in exchange for your talents. If you don't honor and value your talents, no one else will either. If you compromise your self-worth and integrity, others will gladly go along with you. Discover and preserve your distinctiveness.

At the end of this chapter, list your talents and decide how you can use them to help others. When you determine this, find out what others are seeking and if it is in alignment with your talents then let them know that what you have to offer will help them. While others may sense your value, you cannot take it for granted that others will automatically know what it is, therefore you literally have to explain that what you have to offer will make their lives better. Lead others in the direction you are going, to provide a clear picture for them.

Individuals embrace new concepts best when it is presented in story form. Think of things that have happened in your life that relates to how you have helped others, and from your illustration, others will relate to you.

If you find that what you have to offer really does not have value for someone, just exercise non-attachment and let that person go. This will create a space for someone who can use your gifts. When I was in sales I thought I had to sell everyone, so I would constantly call those that kept indicating they were not interested. I kept forcing the issue and using a tremendous amount of energy trying to get them to buy. After using the secrets in this book, I realized that I only needed to focus on my desires and my creative mind would attract new options for me. My life became easier as I was connecting with those who were really interested in what I had to offer.

If you continually compare yourself with others, you will find that some will be more talented than you, while others may not. Understand that this is self-defeating behavior, because you are focusing on outside sources. Focus within on what *you* have to offer, and your feelings of inadequacy will disappear on their own.

You are denying your own qualities and values, if you try to emulate others. Those who copy others will never achieve greatness, in fact, you can't attain mastery by copying someone else, or sticking to old beliefs.

Also, help others to see their own talents and values. We tend to live up to what others think and say about us. Look for the best in others, and encourage them to be everything they can be.

If someone is giving you a hard time pay attention to this, as that person may be helping you in a way that you don't yet recognize. This next story will help convey my meaning. A friend of mine wanted to sign up to sell products for a specific marketing program. In order to do this, she had to send in $175.00 for an administrative fee and start up materials. She completed her application, and off she went to an office supply store that mailed items out Federal Express. The clerk took one look at the address on the letter and said, "My boss won't let me send this out," to which she replied, "Why not"? The clerk became very surly, and said he didn't have to explain himself. He said again that he just wasn't going to mail her package out. The next day she went back in, and asked how she, the clerk, and the manager of the store could work together to get her package out. The clerk told her to give him the package, and he would check with his "Boss" when he came in. Now, my friend had to wait another day, making this three days to find out if her package went out. The "Boss" decided to comply with her request, even though as he put it, "The company was a farce". The package was mailed, and within in two weeks time the company was out of business. Look for clues when others are giving you a hard time. It may be a way for your creative mind to attract your attention, so you will step back, and take another look. Remember, the things that are in alignment with your desires will come to you effortlessly.

When you are defensive about something in your life, i.e., lack of money, physical attractiveness, or low self-worth, someone will surely point this out to you. Your creative mind will not miss an opportunity to bring to your awareness those areas you need to work on. Whatever you have an attachment to will be brought to your attention, time after time.

Keep in mind that whatever you resist, persists, whether it is the words or actions of another. You are giving others a tremendous amount of your energy when you worry, or argue about what they think or say. Let them have their beliefs, and accept that what *you* think or believe is all that counts. If you are envious, critical, jealous, resentful or harbor hate toward another, you are not living in the present moment. These feelings are memories from some *past* event, so think your way through your feelings to neutralize them. When you focus on thoughts and words that no longer serve you, it depletes your energy. So, keep your energy for yourself, and help only those that are in alignment with your purpose.

Learn to live in the present moment, become more lighthearted, and less serious about life. When you are young at heart, you can attract more abundance into your life and others will just seem to gravitate toward you. You want to become as lighthearted as a little child, to bring back the fun and laughter into your own life. To watch little children at play will show you how they are very present with each other, and that when they play they interact, rather than react to each other.

"A dream that will need all the love you can give.
Everyday of your life, for as long as you live."
–Rodgers and Hammerstein

Also enjoy everything you have, including your money. When you use your money, think of it as giving love, whether it is paying bills, buying milk, clothing, etc. The money is merely a form of exchange, so feel as though it is a symbol of your love when you use it. You want to stop feeling separated from your money when you make purchases, and begin to think of it as investing in yourself. You are also allowing the other person to serve you, and in turn they are given something for their energy. In fact, every time we give to someone we are really giving to ourselves, remember what goes around comes around.

WEALTH MAGNETIZER!

1.   Make a list of all your talents, skills and accomplishments, as far back as childhood. List what makes you distinctive; what makes you different; what makes you special; what value you can offer others. If you had a paper route, write it down, if you learned to read easily, write it down, or if you made doll clothes, write it down. Everything you have done in your life required creativity, imagination, and conscious thought.

I was five years of age when I started my first entrepreneurial venture. As you begin listing your skills, many of you will find that you too started ventures early in life. I contacted those that I felt were interested, and in a position to invest [Mom and Dad] in my newly thought up venture [the concession business – lemonade]. This turned out to be the perfect idea, because not only did I receive the capital I needed to establish my business, but I also found my investors played a dual role in my life. Much to my great fortune, they also became my suppliers [lemonade, glasses, pitcher and table].

I then went about organizing my first sales team [my sister and two friends]. We set to work making our sign, and also finding a suitable location to set up business [the sidewalk in front my home].

I left my team to manage the business, while I hit the road calling on potential customers, and by the end of two hours all of our neighbors had purchased our lemonade; we were completely sold out!

I had listed this for a number of years as my first business venture on my resume, and I did indeed get quite a response from potential employers. Now, I am exaggerating but as you may understand this involved imagination and creativity, which *everyone*, not just a few have within them – all you need to do, is to tap into it!

2. Take a week or more to complete this exercise, and don't leave anything out. This exercise will not only have you consciously begin your creative thinking, but this is a way to acknowledge all your achievements and accomplishments – great and small! Look at your list often, as this will indeed reaffirm, how talented and creative you really are.

3. Now highlight three major talents, skills or abilities that you feel would be a fun and creative to make money. There may be latent creative talents that you have not used in years, so begin to consciously decide how you will integrate these into your life. When you start to see your desires becoming fulfilled, this will definitely show you that you can express yourself while creating wealth doing it! Keep in mind that you are not limited to only three creative ways to achieve your goals. This is just a beginning to get those creative thoughts flowing!

4. Listed below are some ideas to get you started!

ABiLiTiES

business	mechanical	artistic/painting/sculpturing
selling	negotiation	management
accounting	coaching	speaking
communication	restoring items	health/medical
listening	financial	entertainment
organizational	brain-storming	administrative

TALENTS

intuition	musical	writing
dancing	arts	designing
cooking	gardening	singing
athletics	acting	helping people
love of children	humor	love of animals

KNOWLEDGE

Chef	Cars	Animals
Tailoring	Horticulture	Psychology
Arts	Wood-crafting	Teaching
Computers	Medical	Sales
Financial	Aerospace	Industry
Travel	Science	Marine/water
Hotel	Athletics	Nature/outdoor sports
Religion	Spirituality	Caregiver

This is a limited list but it gives you ideas, and from the list you can expand further. What area would you be involved in concerning music for example; electronically, playing, organizing, writing, singing, or teaching, the list continues ad infinitum? Continue to creatively think of all the ways that you can integrate what you love into your work. Everyone is highly creative, however it may take some time and effort to unearth those creative abilities, and qualities that exist within you.

5.   Ask yourself – how am I distinctive?

6.   What special qualities can I bring to my relationships – work, social and personal?

7.   List people who have been in your life – all current and past relationships – those who have been in your life from day one. These people can help you create wealth. Ask yourself how you can access them, and how you can create value for them, and for yourself?

Parents/friends   Co-workers/spouses
Siblings/friends   Employers/friends
Teachers/coaches   Business/customers
Friends/friends   Neighbors/friends
Acquaintances/friends   Mentors

Feel the Joy of Money!

You have just won the Lottery AND YOU'RE RICH!

This is a chance to promote a heightened awareness of how it feels to have a tremendous amount of money!

Find a comfortable chair to sit in, and now relax.

Close your eyes, and in your imagination, feel as though there is money scattered all over the room.

Still keeping your eyes closed, imagine sitting right in the middle of all that money!

Feel the joy in your heart about having so much money!

Now, imagine that you are a child again. Jump up and down and up and down, throwing huge amounts of money in the air.

Laugh, giggle and enjoy your great wealth!

Mirror Mirror On The Wall
Who's The Fairest of Them All?

This is an excellent exercise to build your self-image. Very often we feel uncomfortable looking at ourselves in the mirror for any length of time. And many times we feel very self-conscious, while in the presence of others. This technique will change all of that, if you will faithfully practice it!

Choose several of the affirmations from the "Enhance Your Awareness" list. For ten minutes, repeat the affirmations out loud while looking into the mirror. This will help you to become more present when you are with others, and to be more comfortable with who you are. Also make an audio tape of your own voice using the affirmations.

You'll build your self-image while creating tremendous energy, and transformation within you!

15

Your
Source
Of
Power!

"Meditation is not a search; it's not a seeking,
a probing, an exploration.
It is an explosion and discovery."
–Krishnamurti

Meditation is one of the most beneficial techniques used, to keep our mind one pointed and to enhance our ability to focus our attention. One of its greatest values, is its contribution to the expansion of consciousness. When our consciousness expands, new levels of awareness are unlocked; we know that the full development of awareness, is the basis for a successful life.

Meditation creates a form of alchemy, just like the alchemist transforms base metal into gold, meditation can help you discover the elixir of life, by transforming the ordinary state of consciousness into a heightened state of awareness. When we meditate, we connect with our inner wisdom, the source of all our thoughts and desires; we get in touch with who we are, pure unbounded awareness. Through meditation, we can increase our learning ability, our intelligence level, our creativity, our originality, our adaptability, our intuition, etc. In other words, we become so aware that we can make better choices, and realize that what we choose creates our reality. If through the practice of meditation, our lives become such that every pure thought is instantly externalized, we would know as the alchemist does that we can master every event in our lives! We have become the alchemist!

The brain consists of two seemingly separate hemispheres, positioned side by side and connected at the base of the head. Each hemisphere plays a specific role; the right side is considered creative and imaginative, while the left side is considered linear or logical. The brain waves of both hemispheres are not usually in sync with each other; they seem to compete. The purpose of meditation, is to synchronize the brain waves to produce coherency, and when brain waves are coherent, they function in a more organized pattern. This then creates prime conditions for consciousness to fulfill your desires. If you were to introduce the seeds of your desire at the time when your mind seemed to be completely blank, you would experience your dreams and desires instantly.

When water changes into ice, it becomes crystallized, which is a more organized pattern of molecules. Meditation can help us organize our thoughts in much the same way. It allows us to change the set pattern of our thoughts to create more coherency. When our thoughts are coherent, this leads to greater creativity, and purer experiences. Events seem to accelerate and take place effortlessly, and our desires seem to be fulfilled more easily.

When our thoughts are chaotic or random, we are not experiencing full brain wave coherence. Ideally, you want to clear your mind every day of the barrage of thoughts you continually have. How can you introduce new thoughts and ideas, if you are always thinking the same thoughts, or having a multitude of conflicting thoughts? Most people exercise little control over their thoughts, and have what I call *rush hour traffic* going on in their minds.

To tame those thoughts that are running inside your mind like a herd of wild horses, take some time to create silence in your life. Meditation provides the needed silence that not only your conscious mind needs, but your body needs also. Allowing certain stresses to be released so that the assimilation of the day's activities can occur, is a great benefit of meditation.

"Be still and know that I *am* God."
–Psalm 46:10

There is great wisdom in silence – when you pray you are seeking an answer about something in your life, but when you become still or silent, you allow the answers to come to you, therefore silence can provide you with tremendous insight and clarity. Silence holds the secrets and knowledge that you can use to create fulfillment in your life – go into the silence to unravel any problems or mysteries you want solved. After becoming quiet, this is the time you can also focus your attention on thoughts that contain your dreams and desires.

There are many forms of meditation, so select the method that best suits you. A mindfulness meditation technique is given at the end of this chapter that

156

you can use to help quiet the mind. Meditation has a cumulative effect, so keep working with it, and know that since your mind has been given free reign, it may be challenging at first. Continue to practice meditation, and you will definitely feel the difference it makes. The more you meditate, the more freedom you will experience, and ultimately that is what you really want, freedom to be who you want to be, do what you want to do, and create what you want to create.

Getting in touch with who you are through meditation, shows you that you are not just your thoughts rather, you are a silent witness, a silent presence who thinks the thoughts. As you discover this, you will know that you are not just the roles you play; doctor, lawyer, fireman, chief, mother, father, daughter or son, but that you are much, much more. Your true essence is Universal Consciousness; a real force – a force that you have ignored because of your lack of understanding. When you become conscious of how you are an individual expression of Universal Consciousness, you will gain tremendous power to achieve your goals spontaneously.

Most individuals live within the limited idea of themselves, and they have been unaware of their greater dimensional Self or Spirit. Therefore it is not a question of whether you are spiritual or for that matter, spiritual enough to create fulfillment in your life; you are already spiritual so everything you need is right at your fingertips.

There is tremendous power in your focused thought and tremendous power in the present moment to create synchronicity and to create that which seems impossible. If you have come this far through the book and are not just reading the last page, you are already experiencing enlightenment, an expanded state of awareness and increased power to start bringing in the magic!

Remember, if you can dream it – you can do it! Listen to your inner wisdom – it is your secret power – it is the voice of your own soul!
You are here to experience Life! Enjoy it! Love it! Feel it! Master it!
And above all believe in the
Magic of it!

A MINDFULNESS MEDITATION TECHNIQUE

Find a comfortable and quiet place to sit. Close your eyes, and begin to focus on your breath.

Continue to gently focus on your breath – if you notice that your attention drifts toward any thoughts, gently bring your attention back to your breath. You want to go back and forth between your breath, and thoughts very gently.

Meditation is done to quiet the mind, and interrupt your stream of consciousness, so that you can advance to the source of your thoughts. Meditation allows you to release built up stress, and to clear your mind of many unwanted thoughts. Remember you do not meditate to see flashy blue lights, or for extraordinary occurrences during the meditation. You want to connect with the silence that is already within you, so that your everyday activity becomes more peaceful and joyful. If your life is becoming more joyful, and you are experiencing greater and greater good in your life than the meditation is working.

Meditate focusing on your breath for about ten minutes, and after your meditation is complete, choose twelve words from the "Enrich Your Essence & Energy" list. Each word is to be repeated silently in your mind while consciously feeling how it resonates with you. You can also choose to focus your attention on several phrases listed under "Enhance Your Awareness" list. These two exercises are very powerful in capturing your attention, and will greatly enhance your meditation.

CONTRACT

LIST THREE TECHNIQUES YOU HAVE LEARNED FROM "CONSCIOUSLY CREATING WEALTH" THAT YOU WILL PRACTICE EVERY DAY FOR ONE MONTH. IF YOU MISS A DAY, YOU HAVE TO PUT $10 INTO A COOKIE JAR, AND THEN SEND IT TO ME! (I'M JUST KIDDING) HOWEVER, BE DEDICATED TO INTEGRATING THE SECRETS YOU HAVE LEARNED FOR AT LEAST A MONTH. THIS WILL GIVE YOU A SOLID BASE TO WORK FROM. BE SURE TO SIGN AND DATE THE CONTRACT BELOW!

1.

2.

3.

X _____

DATED _____

16

Create
Your
Own
Study
Group

A study group gives you very valuable ways to share, explore, discuss, and expand on the secrets for wealth, wisdom, and success in the "Consciously Creating Wealth" course book. When creating your study group, use the following information merely as a guideline, explore all the infinite probabilities, and make adjustments according to whatever the group desires. The goal of your study group is to come together to expand your thinking, increase your depth of study, get to know each other, yourselves, and have fun doing it!

OK! Let's Get Started!

WHO ORGANIZES THE GROUP?

The person who organizes the study group will find a location, set meeting times, and be responsible for communicating with other group members. Generally it is best to schedule a two-hour session, to meet regularly once a week. A seven-week study group works best, as this gives members time to use, and integrate the material. At the end of each session, review and make plans for the next session.

WHO WILL LEAD THE DISCUSSION?

This person can volunteer to lead a group discussion, or the group can appoint a person after each meeting. This person guides the meeting by leading the discussion, and activities.

CAN NEW PEOPLE JOIN AT ANY TIME?

You may want to add new people at any time, or only at the beginning of your study group. If you decide on a general group discussion each time, it would be easy to include individuals at any time. However, if your group plans on being progressive and beginning each meeting with the next subject in the book, then you will probably want to have people join your study group at the very start.

GETTING ACQUAINTED

Have each person introduce themselves, share their desires, background, experiences, and what specifically brought them to the meeting.

YOUR FIRST MEETING

Begin discussion on the introduction. Turn to the interactive exercise titled, "What are my feelings about money"? Ask each person to give their feelings regarding the four questions listed, and have everyone take enough time to express themselves.

Having an easel would be very beneficial during the "For Or Against" exercise. Draw a line down the middle of the board, on one side write For, and on the other write Against. Ask members to give you answers concerning who is for, and who is against wealth? What are the benefits, and what are the obstacles? Write the answers down, and also determine if the answers are universal, or individual.

Now have everyone complete the exercise, "Feature Article". This is a really fun way to encourage creativity, as well as show each member the potential they have residing within themselves. Have everyone read, and show their "Feature Article" to the group.

Turn to the exercise, "It's In The Cards" and read through the exercise together. The members can complete the exercise at the meeting, or they can do it at home, but impress upon everyone to complete, "It's In The Cards" and be ready to share with the group at the next meeting. Now, review the exercise, "Now That's Synchronicity!" and have members be aware of spontaneous events that take place in their life, for the next week. Also, have members read the next two chapters for the upcoming meeting.

YOUR SECOND MEETING

Have members introduce themselves again, and begin discussion by sharing the previous week's experiences. Ask everyone if they have completed the "It's in The Cards" exercise, and if they have their cards taped everywhere? Now have members take turns sharing their experiences, related to the exercise, "Now that's Synchronicity"! The group will automatically begin to guide itself, but remember to stay on focus, and keep the meeting on an experiential level, so that it provides a chance for everyone to participate. The leader should encourage everyone to share their insights, and experiences.

Now pair off, and take ten minutes to complete the "No Words Spoken Here" exercise. In five minutes change roles with your partner. Again, have members share their feelings about this exercise.

You may want to do something symbolic, or special to close each meeting. You can end each meeting with a special quotation, song, group hug, meditation, or you can have each member take turns composing something unique for each meeting.

YOUR FOLLOWING MEETINGS

By now, everyone is creating a bond, and feeling comfortable with each other. Continue your discussions, and completing the interactive exercises. You may even think of your own interactive exercises that compliment a chapter. Just stay focused at each meeting, be flexible, and be cognizant that everyone has a chance to participate and share. The interaction allows you to fully integrate the material, which in turn will help you focus your energies to bring about fulfillment!

NOTES

NOTES

NOTES

NOTES